The
POINT-TO-POINT
Recruits 2021/2022

Jodie Standing

Published by
Marten Julian
69 Highgate, Kendal,
Cumbria, LA9 4ED
01539 741 007

rebecca@martenjulian.com
www.martenjulian.com

MARTEN JULIAN

1970 • 2021

Marten Julian (Publisher)
69 Highgate, Kendal, Cumbria LA9 4ED
www.martenjulian.com

First published in Great Britain in 2021

Copyright © Jodie Standing

A CIP catalogue record of this book is available from the British Library.

ISBN
978-1-8382317-8-1

ISSN
2633-2418 (Print)

Book Design & layout
Steve Dixon

Photo Credits:
Tattersalls, Jack & Tom Williams of JTW Equine Photography, Neale Blackburn Photography, Craig Payne, Susie Cahill & Jodie Standing.

Disclaimer: Every effort has been made to ensure the accuracy of the information in this publication. Any views or opinions represented in this publication are personal and solely those of the author and do not represent those of trainers, jockeys or connections, unless otherwise clearly stated. Neither the publisher nor author can accept responsibility for errors or omissions, particularly if a horse has run after the publication went to print.

Introduction

Firstly, let me start by thanking you for purchasing this fourth edition of *The Point-To-Point Recruits*. Your support is greatly appreciated and without you this publication would not be possible. I hope the information within proves a useful source of reference for the coming season and beyond.

There was a time this year where I thought a publication devoted to point-to-pointers wouldn't be possible, purely due to the fact that no racing between the flags took place for almost four months. However, once I started my research, I was pleasantly surprised at the quality on offer and I have put together a list of 86 lightly raced individuals from both the British and Irish fields, and amongst those are a special twenty whom I deem to have 'star potential'. This does not necessarily mean I think they'll end up competing in Graded races, but I do believe they'll do especially well for their new connections, at whatever level that may be.

Unlike with horses who have raced under Rules, the point-to-point footage is not the most accessible and many of you will be seeing these names for the first time. With this book I am trying to fill that void in the hope that it may give us a slight edge and earn us some profit along the way.

Last year I added a feature called 'The Look Back', in which I expressed my thoughts on the recruits in the previous year's book. This year I'll be doing the same and pointing out the horses which I believe look well handicapped or can thrive for a switch to hurdles or fences. I also give an indication of their possible long-term targets.

As always, I would like to take this opportunity to thank Marten Julian for being a constant support. I am also indebted to Rebecca Julian-Dixon, Steve Dixon, Ian Greensill, Alessandro Claus and everyone who took time to answer my queries at various stages along the way.

I also must say a special thank you to the photographers who have provided such wonderful images for this publication: Tattersalls, Jack & Tom Williams of JTW Equine Photography, Neale Blackburn Photography and Craig Payne.

Finally, it just leaves me to say that I hope everyone has a successful, enjoyable and, most importantly, safe National Hunt season.

Best wishes,

Jodie Standing

The following horses have all shown sufficient ability or potential to suggest they can make an impact under Rules for their new connections. As is the case with any horse, they will thrive at different stages of their careers. It may take time before some of them fulfil their potential while others may be precocious enough to win bumpers and novice hurdles this season.

AMERICAN MIKE
4YO BAY GELDING

TRAINER:	Gordon Elliott
PEDIGREE:	Mahler – American Jennie (Lord Americo)
FORM:	1 -
OPTIMUM TRIP:	2m +
GOING:	Soft

American Mike is a well-bred individual and looked a class above his opposition when cruising to an emphatic success on debut in a four-year-old geldings' maiden at Cork back in April.

Sean Doyle's gelding always moved smoothly on the heels of the leader and although plenty of the ten runners still held a chance after the fourth from home, American Mike made a bold challenge on the run to the next, moving off the inside rail and forging a passage between horses before a good leap saw him land with a narrow advantage.

A shake of the reins upon landing saw the Mahler gelding extend his lead on the short run to the next where another measured leap took him further clear with a two-length margin quickly turning into eight by the time he'd reached the last. One final assured jump guaranteed the race was in safekeeping as he readily extended up the run-in to cross the line with 20 easy lengths to spare over High Class Hero with a further three-length break to Card Dealer, who was beaten only three parts of a length on his next run.

American Mike is the fifth foal out of American Jennie, a very useful chaser up to 2m 6f – dam of James Moffatt's winning hurdler One Fine Man and point winner Spendajennie.

Sold for £195,000 at Cheltenham's April Sale to Eddie O'Leary acting on behalf of Noel and Valerie Moran's Bective Stud.

American Mike is blessed with a turn of foot but with a pedigree littered with stamina, he could prove useful over a range of trips.

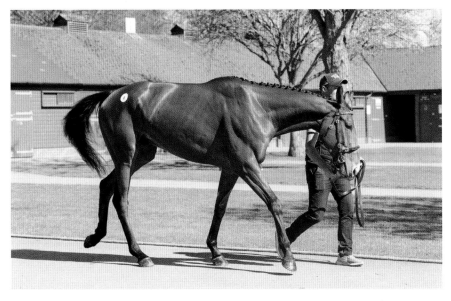

American Mike – parading before fetching £195,000 at the sales (photo by Tattersalls)

ANOTHER MYSTERY
4YO BAY GELDING

TRAINER:	Lucy Wadham
PEDIGREE:	Norse Dancer – Misstree Pitcher (Relief Pitcher)
FORM:	1 -
OPTIMUM TRIP:	2m
GOING:	Good To Soft

A lovely young horse to join Lucy Wadham.

Another Mystery made his English pointing debut in a 14-runner maiden over three miles at Kimble in April for Tom Ellis and Jack Andrews. Sent to the front from the drop of the flag, the field couldn't lay a glove on the Norse Dancer gelding for the majority of the contest as he jumped like a stag and went further clear with each spring-heeled leap.

Only at the fifth and fourth last, when fatigue started to set in, did he make a semblance of a mistake, but that did little to interrupt his impetus as he continued to scorch the turf. Turning for home the distress signals started to flare but to his great credit he pinged the last and managed to keep enough up his sleeve to hold off the late rattle from Dash Full Of Cash who finished with a real surge having been outpaced.

Another Mystery is a half-brother to the point-to-point bumper winner Misstree Song, who later placed in bumpers and over hurdles (2m) for Dan Skelton. His dam is a point winner and placed over hurdles (2m 2f-3m) and is a half-sister to point/2m 4f-3m hurdle/chase winner Misstree Dancer.

Purchased for £55,000 at Cheltenham's April Sale by Lucy Wadham. She also bought the runner-up at the same sale for £45,000.

Another Mystery looks a real speed machine who could easily land a bumper for his new connections.

ANYHARMINASKING
4YO BAY GELDING

TRAINER:	Jonjo O'Neill
PEDIGREE:	Getaway – Collen Beag (Mountain High)
FORM:	1 -
OPTIMUM TRIP:	2m +
GOING:	Good To Soft

This €44,000 store horse made his debut in a four-year-old geldings' maiden for Donnchadh Doyle at Tipperary in April and battled bravely to success at the first time of asking.

Jumping well and tracking the pace-setter for the majority of the race, the gelding made a deliberate challenge for the lead approaching the fourth from home, quickening into the wings of the fence before touching down alongside Constitution Hill. From there, the pair broke away from the field and continually upped the ante over the next couple of fences before turning into the straight still locking horns.

With a better leap coming from his rival over the penultimate fence, Anyharminasking looked as though he'd been put in his place, but after the leader made a terrible blunder at the last, the advantage was gifted back to this gelding who kept on bravely on the run-in despite the eventual runner-up doing his best to stage a rally in the final strides.

There really was no hiding place for the front two in the latter stages of this race, and it's to their great testament that they were able to keep going so bravely to the line. That didn't go unnoticed by prospective buyers as this gelding was purchased for €145,000 by Equos at the Goffs Punchestown Sale in April and now enters training with Jonjo O'Neill.

Out of the four-time course winner Collen Beag (bumper/2m hurdle) who is a half-sister to the useful 2m hurdle winner Noah And The Ark.

Anyharminasking looks to possess the requisite pace to land a bumper before going hurdling.

ASH TREE MEADOW
5YO BAY GELDING

TRAINER:	Gordon Elliott
PEDIGREE:	Bonbon Rose – Alzasca (Grape Tree Road)
FORM:	61 -
OPTIMUM TRIP:	2m +
GOING:	Good To Soft

This is a horse sharp enough to make his presence felt in bumpers.

Ash Tree Meadow shaped like a smart horse on his debut for Donnchadh Doyle at Lisronagh last November, making a good move from the rear before tiring after the last, eventually crossing the line in sixth place, 21 lengths behind the impressive winner, Jim Key, who has since been purchased by Hamish Macauley for an eye-watering £215,000.

Forced to take an extended break due to lockdown restrictions, Ash Tree Meadow reappeared at Fairyhouse in April to compete in the warmly contested 16-runner second division of the geldings' maiden. Clearly thriving from his holiday, the five-year-old travelled strongly on the bridle and moved through to lead with an excellent leap over the third from home before taking a chance at the next. Moving away unscathed and bursting clear with an impressive turn of foot, he opened up a healthy advantage by the time he'd reached the last, which he jumped nimbly before careering up the run-in to record an eased-down 12-length victory over Sean Doyle's more experienced runner, Since Day One.

There was no fluke about this performance, which not only left a lasting visual impression, but it also clocked a time seven seconds quicker than the first division won by Universal Dave.

Purchased by Aidan O'Ryan and Gordon Elliott for £135,000, this son of Bonbon Rose is out of the French 1m 5f winner Alzasca who is a half-sister to

Pacha Du Polder. He is also a half-brother to the useful 2m 3f-2m 4f hurdle/chase winner Darcy Ward.

Ash Tree Meadow is blessed with a tremendous number of gears and although his pedigree leans towards stamina, he looks sure to make his mark in bumpers should connections choose to start him there.

AU FLEURON
4YO BAY GELDING

TRAINER:	Gordon Elliott
PEDIGREE:	Crillon – La Pelodette (Sagamix)
FORM (P2P NHF):	1 -
OPTIMUM TRIP:	2m +
GOING:	Soft

☆ **STAR POTENTIAL** ☆

Here's another top-class prospect to join Gordon Elliott in the colours of Noel and Valerie Moran of Bective Stud having sold at Cheltenham's March Sale for £220,000.

The Crillon gelding was a class apart from his ten rivals in a 2m 2f point-to-point bumper at Tipperary back in March with the eye constantly drawn to him as he travelled powerfully in the mid-division before making smooth headway on the bridle to lead off the turn for home.

Quickly asserting but pricking his ears and showing some signs of inexperience, he knuckled down in ready style passing the two-furlong marker, quickening in response to a few cracks of the whip and seeing the race out strongly up the run-in to cross the line with four and a half lengths to spare over Zero Tolerance.

Au Fleuron hails from a good family and is a half-brother to Coachman who won a point-to-point for the same handler, Denis Murphy, earlier this year and is now in training with Oliver Signy. His dam, La Pelodette, didn't show much when racing in France but she's a half-sister to the three Emma Lavelle-trained winners Tocca Ferro (bumper and dual 2m Listed hurdle winner), Le Bec (2m 4f-3m hurdle/chase winner) and The Last Night (2m chase winner).

This is a likeable young horse who had reportedly schooled very well for his handler prior to his debut. He could quite easily take in another bumper to gain experience, but I fully expect him to flourish once tackling a distance of ground when embarking on a career over hurdles, and later fences.

BALLYBOUGH NATIVE
5YO BAY GELDING

TRAINER:	Henry de Bromhead
PEDIGREE:	Shirocco – Cullian (Missed Flight)
FORM (P2P NHF):	1 -
OPTIMUM TRIP:	2m 4f +
GOING:	Soft

⭐ **STAR POTENTIAL** ⭐

Henry de Bromhead looks to have added another above-average performer to his stable.

Ballybough Native came home 12 lengths to the good over the subsequent Punchestown Land Rover Bumper fourth, Time Marches On, in a 2m 2f point-to-point bumper at Tipperary in March and in doing so recorded a first racecourse success for handler and professional jockey, Ian McCarthy.

The tempo looked strong from the outset which found out plenty of the 13-strong line-up a long way from home, but Jamie Codd was happy to take his time aboard the Shirocco gelding before picking off the opposition one by one down the back straight. Travelling wide but always going comfortably, Ballybough Native moved into third rounding the turn for home and picked up well when asked to go after the leader. Drawing upon his stamina, he took to the front inside the final two furlongs and pulled away with the minimal amount of fuss on the run to the line, crossing it with his head in his chest and giving favourite backers no cause for concern.

Ballybough Native is a half-brother to the 2m 5f hurdle winner Fourina and point winners Control Me and Clondaw Nell. His dam was a five-time winner over hurdles and fences up to 2m 5f and is a half-sister to Noel Meade's useful 1m-1m 1f Flat/2m and 2m 2f hurdle winner Be My Hope.

Despite the decent amount of pace in Ballybough Native's pedigree, he looks more of a stayer on soft ground. It'll be interesting to see where connections go with him this term, but I imagine a season over hurdles awaits. He's exciting.

BALLYHAWKISH
5YO BAY GELDING

TRAINER:	Neil King
PEDIGREE:	Kayf Tara – Massannie (Dr Massini)
FORM:	1 -
OPTIMUM TRIP:	2m +
GOING:	Soft

★ **STAR POTENTIAL** ★

Ballyhawkish created a favourable impression in a decent standard four-year-olds' maiden at Loughbrickland last November – a race previously won by the likes of Mossy Fen, Plan Of Attack and Benatar.

Sitting towards the rear of the tightly grouped field for much of the race, the four-year-old made progress approaching the fourth from home where a bold leap took him closer to the action. Big over the next, he lost some momentum but picked up in good style after being ridden for a stride or two and produced a momentum-building jump over the penultimate fence which propelled him up the hill before taking the tight bend for home.

Poking his nose to the front and meeting the final fence on a good stride, he then quickened on the descent to the line and stayed on strongly to win by a cosy two and a half lengths in a time ten seconds quicker than standard.

Visually this looked a decent race and the form has held up well with the second, Git Maker, subsequently winning by ten lengths and now resides at Jamie Snowden's having been purchased for £105,000.

Ballyhawkish is the first foal out of Massannie who won four times, including a bumper and three times over hurdles (2m 2f-2m 5f). She is closely related to the 2m-2m 3f hurdle winner Annsam – a winner on both soft and good to firm conditions.

Ballyhawkish's race was on heavy ground, and although he went through it well, I imagine he'd be more at home on a better surface. He's a sharp sort and I'm sure we'll see him running around the tight turns of Fakenham in his first season under Rules.

Neil King – has some useful recruits to look forward to this season (photo by Tattersalls)

BALLYKEEL
5YO BAY GELDING

TRAINER: TBC
PEDIGREE: Presenting – Captain Supreme (Captain Rio)
FORM: 3 -
OPTIMUM TRIP: 2m +
GOING: Good to Soft

Ballykeel hasn't been seen since finishing an admirable third on his pointing debut at Loughbrickland last November but he should be noted once embarking on a career under Rules.

The Presenting gelding made his debut in what looked to be a good four-year-olds' maiden run in very testing conditions. He was never too far from the pace and appeared to be still travelling in his comfort zone until hitting the third from home on the uphill section of the track. Quickly back on an even keel, he then breasted the next and dropped to third, but to his great credit he kept on battling and rounded the tight turn for home with only a length or so to find. A better jump at the last helped his cause, but he couldn't quite find the extra gear needed on the downhill run to the line but kept on at the one pace to finish four lengths adrift of Ballyhawkish, who came with a sweeping run from the rear.

In second was Warren Ewing's Git Maker, who has since franked the form when winning by ten lengths at Necarne.

Ballykeel is a half-brother to three winners – New Age Dawning (bumper/2m 7f hurdle), Higgs (2m 1f hurdle) and Blackstair Rocco (2m 4f hurdle). His dam was an unraced sister to Allure Of Illusion (bumper/2m 4f hurdle) who is a half-sister to Blackstairmountain.

Ballykeel doesn't look a world-beater, but he's a tough and genuine sort, which will stand him in very good stead. A drop back in trip for a bumper, or hurdles over 2m could be the ticket to success. Being by Presenting, he will also probably prefer better conditions to those that he encountered on his debut.

BEAUTE NOIRE
5YO BROWN MARE

TRAINER:	Lucinda Russell
PEDIGREE:	Arcadio – Mrs Gordi (Classic Cliche)
FORM:	2 -
OPTIMUM TRIP:	2m 4f
GOING:	Soft

This striking-looking mare showed good raw ability to fill the runner-up spot on her only start to date.

Beaute Noire is a scopey daughter of Arcadio and was given time to physically develop before making her debut in a five-year-old mares' maiden at Fairyhouse for Graham McKeever. Held up in the rear of mid-division for a good part of the race, the eye was drawn to her as she made steady progress after the fifth from home before a more deliberate challenge was made as she scythed her way through the pack after landing with momentum over the third last.

Looking very green, she made a mistake at the penultimate fence when progressing on to the heels of the leaders but soon picked up for a crack of the whip and charged into the lead around the home bend. Stretching a length or more clear of her nearest pursuer on the run to the last, she appeared to have the race in the bag but lack of maturity got the better of her as she jinked on the approach and landed awkwardly, gifting her advantage to Present Storm who was able to hold on to the line and win by a length and a half.

That form was boosted by the third, Craan Run, who won next time out whilst the winner has shown promise on three of her four starts for Charlie Longsdon.

Purchased for £50,000 at the Goffs UK Spring Sale, Beaute Noire is a half-sister to the bumper/3m hurdle winner Billy Billy and point winner Over Stated. Her dam is an unraced sister to the 2m 4f hurdle/3m 2f chase winner Carnival Town from the family of Stayers' Hurdle winner Anzum.

Clearly blessed with an engine and a decent number of gears, Beaute Noire has the natural ability to make her presence felt in the mares' division this winter. It's possible she could start in a bumper to gain experience, but I expect she'll prove most effective over 2m 4f.

BRAVO TEAM
5YO CHESTNUT GELDING

TRAINER:	TBC
PEDIGREE:	Imperial Monarch – Rapid Heartbeat (Old Vic)
FORM:	P1 -
OPTIMUM TRIP:	2m 4f +
GOING:	Soft/Heavy

A well-bred individual with the stamina to develop into a staying chaser.

Bravo Team made his debut for Colin Bowe in a decent standard four-year-old geldings' maiden at Lingstown last November and appeared to be going well when hitting the front on the final circuit but weakened tamely with three fences to jump and was eventually taken out of the race by Barry O'Neill.

Sent to Dromahane the following month, he atoned for that disappointment in no uncertain terms and returned the easy eight-length winner of the ten-runner contest. The sound-jumping gelding was clearly too good for the field and went to the front as the tapes went back and never looked in any real danger as he readily pulled away from his only challenger after a slick leap over the last.

The form has not worked out well with those in behind well beaten on their subsequent starts, but the time of the race was good and Bravo Team looked cut from a different cloth. He also possesses a great deal of size, has a lovely way of travelling through a race and has foot-perfect precision over his fences.

Out of a half-sister to the outstanding race mare Voler La Vedette, Bravo Team looks a sort to do well under Rules. He has pace and is a half-brother to the bumper winner Howth Summit, but I fully expect him to thrive when covering a distance of ground. He also looked well suited to testing conditions.

CALL HER NOW
4YO BAY FILLY

TRAINER:	Lorna Fowler
PEDIGREE:	Presenting – Denwoman (Witness Box)
FORM:	1
OPTIMUM TRIP:	2m 4f +
GOING:	Good to Soft

From the family of Denman and a half-sister to Willie Mullins' smart bumper winner, Tactical Move.

Call Her Now made a striking debut for Cormac Doyle in a four-year-old mares' maiden at Necarne in mid-May. Only six runners went to post and the race looked an average standard, but this filly was clearly head and shoulders above the field and dominated proceedings after taking up the running from the second fence.

Setting only a modest pace, Call Her Now jumped well and although challenged at the third from home where she pecked slightly on landing, she responded well and demonstrated a bright turn of foot on the run to the next. There she jumped well and gradually re-extended her advantage before the last, again clearing the fence with room to spare, before crossing the line with three and a half lengths in hand over Motown Maggie, who was benefiting from two previous runs.

Being by Presenting, the same sire as Denman, out of a Witness Box mare, Call Her Now has a pedigree that suggests she'll be best suited to trips that bring her stamina into play. That said, she also appears to have bags of natural pace that could be put to good use in a bumper. She may prove versatile with regards to the ground, with her victory coming on a soft surface, but Presenting's progeny generally like better conditions.

Purchased for £240,000 at Cheltenham's May Sale by Rahinston Stud, she will now be trained by Lorna Fowler and is most definitely a name to note.

CAPTAIN QUINT
5YO BAY GELDING

TRAINER:	Rose Dobbin
PEDIGREE:	Flemensfirth – Vics Miller (Old Vic)
FORM:	2 -
OPTIMUM TRIP:	2m 4f +
GOING:	Soft

Rose Dobbin buys some nice prospects, and Captain Quint is right up there.

The eye-filling son of Flemensfirth shaped with great promise when staying on at the one pace behind the very well-regarded Guily Billy on his pointing debut at Tinahely last November.

Ground and weather conditions were atrocious, but Jamie Codd kept the Denis Murphy-trained gelding close to the pace throughout before edging nearer to challenge after the third from home. Moving into second spot with two lengths to find on the pace-setting winner, he did his best to close on the uphill rise to the final couple of fences but despite pulling a long way clear of the third, he couldn't quite latch on to Guily Billy and was eventually beaten four lengths at the line.

That horse has since passed through the ring to Cheveley Park Stud for £310,000 making Captain Quint look good value at £110,000.

A half-brother to the 3m 1f chase winner Speedy Cargo and point winner Bold Conduct. His dam is an unraced half-sister to Maljimar (2m 1f-3m 6f hurdle/chase/cross-country chase).

Captain Quint may start in a bumper to gain experience, but he will come into his own once stepped up in trip to 2m 4f or further. Given his substantial frame, he will need a galloping track to be seen at his best; somewhere like Carlisle or Ayr would suit.

CARLO DU BERLAIS
4YO BAY GELDING

TRAINER:	Fergal O'Brien
PEDIGREE:	Carlotamix – Dark Ebony (Flemensfirth)
FORM:	F2 -
OPTIMUM TRIP:	2m +
GOING:	Soft

An honest sort of horse who looks sure to get off the mark for his new connections.

Carlo Du Berlais was in the midst of running a good race on his debut at Tipperary in April until taking a heavy fall at the third from home when still holding every chance in fourth place. That looked a good standard race with Colin Bowe's winner, Chianti Classico, going on to fetch £105,000 at the Cheltenham Sale 12 days later and now enters training with Kim Bailey whilst the fourth, beaten 28 lengths, and the sixth, Phantom Getaway, both went on to win next time. The latter also enters training with Bailey having been sold for £90,000.

Carlo Du Berlais was turned out over the same course and distance 13 days later, this time finishing second, staying on at the line to be beaten only three lengths by Merry Maker with a six-length break back to Happy Boy in third. A little hesitant over his fences, perhaps remembering the previous mishap, the four-year-old travelled strongly and showed a willing attitude to chase home the eventual winner from the penultimate fence but couldn't find the change of gear needed to get on terms.

This was an encouraging display and the form has worked out well with the seventh winning next time, whilst the sixth and tenth also improved their positions next time out – the latter, Hold Onto The Line, only failing by a length and a half in second and he now enters training with James Ewart.

Carlo Du Berlais is a lovely-moving horse who is well put together and uses himself to great effect. He was purchased for £80,000 by Highflyer Bloodstock on behalf of Owners Group at the Doncaster Spring Sale in May and is now trained by Fergal O'Brien.

Bred for both speed and stamina with connections to 2m 4f hurdle winners and 1m 2f French Flat winners.

I envisage the Carlotamix gelding gaining experience in bumpers but really coming into his own over hurdles when upped in trip to 2m 3f.

Carlo Du Berlais – just one of the many talented young horses to join Fergal O'Brien (photo by JTW Equine Photography)

CHANCYCOURT
5YO BAY GELDING

TRAINER:	Fergal O'Brien
PEDIGREE:	Court Cave – She Saval (Deploy)
FORM:	3 - 2
OPTIMUM TRIP:	2m 4f +
GOING:	Good to Soft

Chancycourt remains a maiden after two tries in points but judging by the potential he showed on both starts it won't be long before he gets off the mark.

The good-looking son of Court Cave made his debut at Tipperary in April, finishing third, 12 lengths behind Mary Doyle's easy winner, Gandhi Maker. Chancycourt raced in the mid-division for a good chunk of the race and made headway on the bridle after the fourth from home but wasn't knocked about by his jockey as the smooth-travelling winner kicked clear.

He then went to Dromahane in early May, this time finishing second to Ted Hastings who has subsequently joined Gordon Elliott for a sum of £68,000. Here Chancycourt raced more prominently and caught the eye travelling well in third place after the fourth from home. Asked to close on the front-running winner, the five-year-old quickly closed the deficit before the penultimate fence before getting within a length of the leader at the last. There he cleared the fence well but couldn't find the extra gear needed to overhaul the winner despite sticking on gamely all the way to the line.

Being by Court Cave out of a Deploy mare and related to several winners up to three miles, Chancycourt will most likely need a trip to be seen at his best. Good ground will suit him well.

He's an exciting addition to Fergal O'Brien's yard.

CHIANTI CLASSICO
4YO BAY GELDING

TRAINER:	Kim Bailey
PEDIGREE:	Shantou – Ballinderry Lady (Presenting)
FORM:	1 -
OPTIMUM TRIP:	2m +
GOING:	Good

Chianti Classico looks well bought by Kim Bailey and Aiden Murphy for £105,000.

The Shantou gelding displayed plenty of natural pace and gears to make a stylish winning debut at Tipperary in April for Colin Bowe and Barry O'Neill. Never too far from the pace, the four-year-old eventually pressed on after the sixth fence and impressed with his nimble and efficient jumping.

Always appearing to be travelling in his comfort zone, the gelding effortlessly upped the tempo and had the field on the stretch approaching the third from home, entering the home straight still on the bridle. Showing a good turn of foot and another quick leap over the penultimate fence, he had the race in safekeeping when taking a chance at the last but came away unscathed before crossing the line with a comfortable two and a half lengths to spare over Stumptown in second.

This was a taking debut from Chianti Classico who appears to possess an athletic frame and bounced off the good to yielding ground. Out of a dam who was an unraced half-sister to Duke Des Champs and related to the high-class staying chaser Harbour Pilot, Chianti Classico has the potential to be a smart sort.

Given his confidence in the air, he could prove very useful over hurdles, especially when encountering good ground. He's not short of pace but also has stamina.

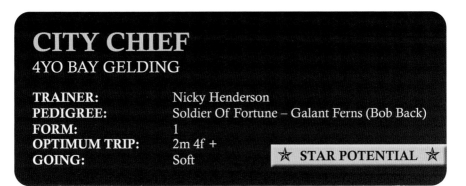

CITY CHIEF
4YO BAY GELDING

TRAINER: Nicky Henderson
PEDIGREE: Soldier Of Fortune – Galant Ferns (Bob Back)
FORM: 1
OPTIMUM TRIP: 2m 4f +
GOING: Soft

★ **STAR POTENTIAL** ★

This is a very exciting individual with stamina in abundance.

City Chief left quite an impression in the four-year-old geldings' maiden at Tralee in late May when given a supremely confident ride by Luke Murphy to win with far more in hand than the three parts of a length suggests.

Always travelling well and catching the eye, the gelding made stealthy progress from the rear of mid-division to sit on the heels of the leaders on the long run to the third from home where he jumped well but didn't land with as much momentum as those around him. Pushed back into the bridle before turning into the straight, the response was good and he soon moved back into third spot and took aim at the leaders.

Foot perfect over the penultimate fence, his jockey was yet to ask for an effort but the gelding started to erode the deficit and met the final fence running, allowing him to push off with momentum which he used to overhaul the two leaders on the short run to the line and win going away.

This really was a race that made you sit up and take notice. City Chief is an imposing individual with an impressive stride and obviously has stamina in abundance to plough through the testing conditions. The time of the race was also impressive, clocking a time 16 seconds quicker than average and a whopping 34 seconds quicker than the four-year-old mares' maiden half an hour earlier. It was also four seconds quicker than the five-year-old geldings' maiden later on the card.

Unsurprisingly he attracted plenty of attention at the sales with the hammer eventually knocking down to a tune of £210,000 with David Minton standing alongside Nicky Henderson responsible for the final bid.

Out of the five-time winner Galant Ferns (bumper/useful 2m 6f-3m 1f hurdle/ chase) who is a half-sister to the useful bumper/2m-2m 4f hurdle/chase winner On Tour. He is also a half-brother to the point/2m 4f hurdle winner Premium Package.

It's possible for City Chief to gain experience in bumpers but I fully expect him to thrive over hurdles when upped in trip to 2m 4f. Ultimately, he looks like an exciting chaser for seasons to come.

City Chief – a cosy winner at Tralee (photo by Tattersalls)

CONSTITUTION HILL
4YO BAY GELDING

TRAINER:	Nicky Henderson
PEDIGREE:	Blue Bresil – Queen Of The Stage (King's Theatre)
FORM:	2 -
OPTIMUM TRIP:	2m
GOING:	Good to Soft

This gelding suffered a race-costing blunder at Tipperary in April.

The good-looking type set a strong pace throughout division one of the four-year-old geldings' maiden and still held a comfortable advantage jumping the fifth from home until joined for the lead by Anyharminasking who quickened upsides approaching the next.

With the pair moving stride for stride over the next couple of fences, there was no place to hide entering the home straight, but this gelding appeared to be getting the upper hand after producing a better leap over the penultimate fence.

Ridden, but holding a length advantage approaching the last, he then met the fence all wrong, almost unshipping his jockey on the landing side and losing all momentum. To his great credit, and also his jockey, who managed to keep the partnership intact, Constitution Hill stayed on well again up the run-in but the line came just in time for the eventual winner who held on by a head.

Constitution Hill was almost certainly an unlucky loser but the fine effort didn't go unnoticed by Nicky Henderson who purchased the gelding at the Goffs UK Spring Sale for £120,000.

A first foal out of the 2m and 2m 2f-winning hurdler Queen Of The Stage who is out of a 2m hurdle winner.

This is a family blessed with plenty of speed and we'll likely see Constitution Hill start in a bumper to gain experience, or in the two-mile hurdle division. He has a lovely attitude.

CONTEMPLATEMYFAITH
5YO BAY GELDING

TRAINER:	Olly Murphy
PEDIGREE:	Califet – Liss A Chroi (Exit To Nowhere)
FORM (P2P NHF):	3 -
FORM:	3 -
OPTIMUM TRIP:	2m 4f +
GOING:	Good to Soft

An eye-catcher on both starts to date.

Contemplatemyfaith made a promising pointing debut on terrible ground at Boulta in December, where despite jumping clumsily, he still managed to plug on to finish a solid third, 20 lengths behind the impressive 12-length winner Setme Straightmate.

The Califet gelding then filled the same position in a point-to-point bumper at Tipperary over an extended 2m 3f. Travelling comfortably in a prominent position throughout but lacking a little tactical pace when the race developed up the home straight, he stayed on strongly close home having been short of room.

Contemplatemyfaith looks to have a good amount of ability and is likely to develop into a stayer – not totally devoid of pace but takes a few strides to find top gear.

He comes from a good family and is a half-brother to J P McManus' useful 2m-3m hurdle/chaser A Great View and 2m hurdler Roll It Out, and also Heated Debate who was successful in points for Francesca Nimmo. His dam is an unraced half-sister to the smart bumper/2m-2m 4f hurdle winner Liss A Paoraigh.

Purchased by Highflyer for £75,000, the five-year-old will now head into training with Olly Murphy for the Owners Group. A campaign over hurdles surely awaits.

COOL SURVIVOR
4YO BAY GELDING

TRAINER:	Gordon Elliott
PEDIGREE:	Westerner – Pale Face (High Chaparral)
FORM:	1 -
OPTIMUM TRIP:	2m +
GOING:	Soft

Cool Survivor made a comfortable winning debut in the hands of Jack Hendrick for handler Cormac Doyle at Cork in April, crossing the line with far more in hand than the four-length beating of Serious Charges would suggest.

Never too far from the pace, the Westerner gelding made an eye-catching move after the fifth from home to take up the running on the run to the next before being outjumped by the Sam Curling-trained Ballycamus. Soon recovering the lost ground, Cool Survivor was then ridden to get back on terms with the leader approaching three out, moving to the front, this time with a better leap, before extending his advantage on the run to the next.

Clearing that well, he then found plenty for gentle pressure on the run to the last and appeared to have matters in full control with one final good leap sealing the deal as he came away readily up the run-in.

Visually this was a nice performance from the four-year-old, and the form looks OK too with the third, beaten over 24 lengths, finishing a four-length second next time. Azof Des Mottes, who unseated when hampered at the penultimate fence, also showed up well on his next two starts when filling the places.

Cool Survivor looks a pacy sort, backed up by his pedigree as his dam, Pale Face, is a half-sister to a German 1m Group 2 winner.

Purchased by Gordon Elliott for £175,000, he should have a say in bumpers this term before being sent hurdling. With High Chaparral on the dam's side, he may be best with a little give underfoot.

CORRIGEEN ROCK
4YO BAY GELDING

TRAINER:	Lucinda Russell
PEDIGREE:	Westerner – Set In Her Ways (Old Vic)
FORM:	1 -
OPTIMUM TRIP:	2m +
GOING:	Good to Soft

Lucinda Russell does very well with her point-to-point purchases and Corrigeen Rock looked a quality sort when making a winning debut at Fairyhouse in April.

The Denis Murphy-trained four-year-old travelled well throughout the three miles and moved to the front with a good leap over the third from home. Pouring on the pressure thereafter, the gelding stretched his advantage with another fluent jump over the next and held a healthy advantage over the field turning for home. After being momentarily challenged when idling, he kicked on again once given a shake of the reins and produced another spring-heeled leap over the last which sent him clear up the run-in to record a fairly impressive four-length success over Colin Bowe's Money Heist.

This was a promising victory which recorded the fastest time set on the day. Clearly not short of speed and appearing to enjoy the good underfoot conditions, it'll be interesting to see if connections, who bought him for £50,000 at Cheltenham's April Sale, start him in bumpers or go straight over hurdles.

A full brother to point winner Set In The West and a half-brother to Nicky Richards' bumper winner Kitty Hall. His dam was a two-time winner for Kim Bailey, including a bumper and a 2m 4f handicap hurdle and is a half-sister to a 2m 6f hurdle winner from the family of Tourist Attraction.

Corrigeen Rock – enjoying a moment of calm at the sales (photo by Tattersalls)

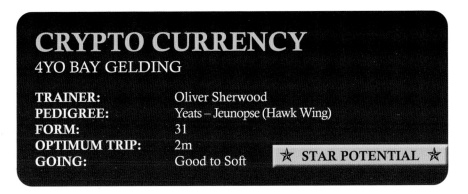

CRYPTO CURRENCY
4YO BAY GELDING

TRAINER:	Oliver Sherwood
PEDIGREE:	Yeats – Jeunopse (Hawk Wing)
FORM:	31
OPTIMUM TRIP:	2m
GOING:	Good to Soft

☆ STAR POTENTIAL ☆

This nimble individual should have no problem lining up in bumpers or in hurdle events over 2m.

Tom Keating's gelding showed bags of natural ability on his debut at Dromahane in May behind Watch House Cross and Garcon Dargent, travelling smoothly and looming up to challenge after the third from home only to weaken after the next and lose his position. It later transpired that he returned home sick.

Typical for a horse from Tom's yard, the gelding improved considerably for that outing and put his experience to good use later in the month at Kirkistown where he demonstrated copious amounts of pace to quicken to the front after the second from home. Not for stopping and with the field unable to go with him, he opened up a considerable advantage by the time he'd reached the final fence before scooting away up the run-in to record an eased-down seven-length success.

The pace of that race was steady from the outset, ultimately putting the emphasis on speed in the latter stages which may not have suited his opposition. However, that shouldn't take anything away from the performance of Crypto Currency who wasn't the quickest or neatest over his fences, but clearly has a huge engine.

From the family of leading jumps sire Beneficial and out of a dam who won on the Flat over 1m 3f and was later placed over hurdles (2m-3m). This gelding looks to have the class and natural speed to make his presence felt in bumpers before embarking on a career over hurdles.

CRYSTAL GLORY
5YO BAY GELDING

TRAINER:	Nicky Richards
PEDIGREE:	Fame And Glory – Nile Cristale (Northern Crystal)
FORM:	11 -
OPTIMUM TRIP:	2m 4f +
GOING:	Soft

Nicky Richards doesn't have many horses in his yard that descend from the Irish pointing field, but here he has a smart-looking recruit who already has two victories to his name.

Crystal Glory could be described as a fortuitous winner when getting off the mark at the first time of asking in a dramatic four-year-old geldings' maiden at Monksgrange last September. After helping to set the pace, the Donnchadh Doyle-trained bay looked destined for fourth place at best after being headed entering the home straight, only for two horses in front of him to fall independently at the penultimate fence before the new leader exited the contest at the last, leaving Crystal Glory to come home one and a half lengths in front of the staying-on Gortmillish – the only other finisher from the ten that started – who went on to win a point and place twice under Rules in bumpers for Denise Foster.

Given a chance to prove himself, Crystal Glory then went for a 'Winner Of One' race the following month at Tattersalls Farm, which he won easily by three lengths from Diegos Way, travelling strongly and picking off the long-time leader with the minimal amount of fuss entering the straight before seeing out the race strongly.

A half-brother to Oliver Sherwood's 2m-2m 4f hurdle/chase winner Morning Reggie, his dam is a French hurdle/chase winner over 2m 1f and is a half-sister to the French 2m 4f Listed chase winner Nile Bonheur and 2m 1f hurdle/chase winner Nile Glorieuse.

Crystal Glory looks a classy recruit to join Greystoke and has the physical scope and potential to develop into an above-average performer when his stamina is tested.

Crystal Glory – building up his fitness in the Cumbrian fells (photo by Jodie Standing)

DANCING WITH DECO
5YO BROWN GELDING

TRAINER:	Alastair Ralph
PEDIGREE:	Milan – Miss Toulon (Toulon)
FORM:	3/2
OPTIMUM TRIP:	2m +
GOING:	Soft

Dancing With Deco wasn't disgraced when finishing 19 lengths behind Bareback Jack on his pointing debut for Liam Kenny at Punchestown in February 2020, matching strides with the eventual winner until blowing up when heads turned for home.

That winner has proved to be very useful, winning three times for Donald McCain and achieving a mark over hurdles of 136. The second that day also looks OK having joined Neil Mulholland as he's filled the places on four of his five races under Rules and achieved a mark over hurdles of 112.

Dancing With Deco stayed in the pointing field and reappeared at Dawstown in May, this time for handler Harley Dunne and finished three lengths adrift of the potentially useful Frontline Citizen with four lengths to spare over the third, Moore On Tour.

Dancing With Deco sat just off the pace but moved closer to the action approaching the third from home, where a good jump saw him poke his nose into a narrow advantage. Ridden along to maintain his position, he was headed at the next but battled on well and cleared the last nicely before keeping on at the one pace to the line.

Despite having influences of stamina on both sides of his pedigree with Milan and Toulon, Dancing With Deco shapes like a horse in need of a shorter trip, possibly 2m 4f or even 2m. His half-brother Miss Me Now was a winner over hurdles (2m) having won on bumper debut for Willie Mullins. His dam was also a bumper winner before gaining success over hurdles (2m & 2m 4f) and is a half-sister to the smart chaser Little Josh.

This looks like a really solid purchase to join Alastair Ralph for £55,000. There ought to be plenty of fun to be had with him.

DONNY BOY
5YO BAY GELDING

TRAINER:	Nick Alexander
PEDIGREE:	Westerner – Lady Roania (Saddlers' Hall)
FORM:	1 -
OPTIMUM TRIP:	2m 4f +
GOING:	Soft

A full brother to the yard's bumper and hurdle winner Ebony Jewel.

Donny Boy created a good impression when powering clear to make a winning debut in the first division of the four-year-old geldings' maiden at Dromahane in December for handler Aidan Fitzgerald and jockey Harley Dunne, stopping the clock 16 seconds quicker than standard and five seconds faster than the second division.

Travelling strongly in mid-division for the vast majority of the race, the gelding was cajoled along to close on the leaders between the fourth and third from home before moving up to challenge for the lead with a slick jump over the penultimate fence. Staying on strongly and poking his nose to the front over the last, the gelding had plenty left in the tank as he drew clear on the run-in, crossing the line with a widening four-length gap back to the second with another two lengths back to the third.

That form looks OK with both the second and third placing under Rules for their new connections whilst Champ Kiely, who was still in contention when exiting the race at the third from home, made a winning debut in a bumper at Limerick for Willie Mullins.

Donny Boy obviously has a decent amount of pace, but given how strongly he crossed the line, races that bring his stamina into play ought to suit him well. He could be one to watch out for in a soft ground bumper around somewhere like Ayr.

DOOYORK
5YO BAY MARE

TRAINER:	Oliver Greenall
PEDIGREE:	Shantou – Hannah Rose (Un Desperado)
FORM:	S1 -
OPTIMUM TRIP:	2m +
GOING:	Soft

A full sister to Emmet Mullins' smart performer Zero Ten.

Dooyork didn't make the best start to her racing career when slipping up on debut at Lisronagh at the beginning of May but quickly atoned for that mishap only eight days later at Tattersalls Farm when staying on strongly over the final couple of fences to win in good style. That was a competitive contest with 14 runners going to post, most of which had some sort of previous experience.

Dooyork raced in mid-division for a good chunk of the race before being urged to take closer order after the third from home. Quickly on to the heels of the leaders on the short run to the next, she then proceeded to make a deliberate challenge for the lead on the turn into the straight before slightly impeding her two rivals when crossing their paths. Staying on well, she took the final fence in her stride and despite wandering on the run to the line, she had plenty up her sleeve to hold the rallying Time For Bell by a length and a half, with only a head back to the third who went on to frank the form the following week.

Dooyork is well bred being a full sister to the aforementioned Zero Ten, who not only achieved success in bumpers, over hurdles and fences, he also won on the Flat over 1m 4f. She is also a full sister to Do The Floss who won a point and is a half-sister to Oriental Fixer who won a 3m 2f chase.

This is a family that flourishes as they mature, so for Dooyork to have already achieved success says plenty of the natural ability she possesses. She looks very well bought for £40,000 and should provide Oliver Greenall with plenty of fun.

She ought to have enough pace to compete in bumpers, but expect improvement when she tackles hurdles, and later fences.

DREAM IN THE PARK
4YO BAY GELDING

TRAINER:	Emma Lavelle
PEDIGREE:	Walk In The Park – Old Dreams (Old Vic)
FORM:	2
OPTIMUM TRIP:	2m +
GOING:	Soft

This gelding emerged from his debut with great potential.

Dream In The Park made his debut for Cormac Doyle in a warmly contested four-year-olds' maiden at Dromahane in May where he was one of seven newcomers to make up the ten-runner field.

Waited with in the rear for a good chunk of the contest, the gelding made ground on the final circuit and moved on to the heels of the leaders on the long run to the third from home before attempting to burrow up the inside of the eventual winner upon touching down. Forced to snatch up and switch back around Frontier General, to Dream In The Park's great credit he was undeterred in his efforts and battled bravely, jumping the penultimate fence almost alongside the leader and matching their injection of pace on the sprint to the last.

Possibly nosing to the front as the pair touched down together, the gelding did his best but was outstayed in the closing stages and eventually crossed the line one and a half lengths adrift of the winner having pulled ten lengths clear of the third.

This was a gutsy performance by Dream In The Park and had it not been for the interference when angling for room after the third from home, he may have built up enough momentum over the last couple of fences to take him clear.

What we did learn is that he's a horse blessed with a good number of gears which should see him competitive in bumpers. His dam was a bumper winner before staying 3m 1f over fences and she's closely related to the useful 2m 4f-2m 6f hurdle/chase winner Oscar Barton.

He's a nice type.

DUBLIN CALLING
5YO BAY GELDING

TRAINER:	TBC
PEDIGREE:	Shirocco – Go On Eileen (Bob Back)
FORM:	1
OPTIMUM TRIP:	2m +
GOING:	Soft

A well-bred son of Shirocco who looks to have a decent engine.

The Pat Doyle-trained Shirocco gelding displayed a willing attitude when making a winning debut in a five-year-olds' maiden at Punchestown in May. Never too far from the pace, he jumped well and showed good pace to quicken a few lengths clear off the home bend before being headed over the last when Paudie, who was finishing with a real rattle from the rear, was quicker through the air and touched down with momentum.

Staying on determinedly, Dublin Calling dug deep and regained the lead inside the final 100 yards, eventually crossing the line with more in hand than the two-length margin gives him credit for.

Dublin Calling is the seventh foal out of the 3m-winning hurdler Go On Eileen – dam of the smart bumper and later 2m-3m hurdle/chase winner Regal Encore, bumper/2m 3f-3m useful hurdler The Organist and point/bumper and 3m hurdle winner Marilyn Monroe.

With such a successful family, this €68,000 store horse ought to have a successful career under Rules. Given his round knee action, I would think he'll be most at home on a soft surface, and I would hope he'd have enough pace for a bumper, should connections choose to go down that avenue. He will stay a trip in time.

EMMA BLUE
4YO BAY FILLY

TRAINER:	Oliver Greenall
PEDIGREE:	Mahler – Rhapsody In Blue (Winged Love)
FORM:	1
OPTIMUM TRIP:	2m +
GOING:	Good to Soft

This gutsy daughter of Mahler could have a lucrative time in the mares' division.

Emma Blue appeared to possess a good deal of pace when making a successful debut for owner/trainer Harley Dunne in the four-year-old mares' maiden at Ballingarry towards the end of May. Given a good ride by Tiernan Power Roche, the mare jumped well and travelled strongly throughout the three miles before making a race-winning move when ridden to lead approaching the turn into the straight.

Quickening in response to her jockey's urgings, she caught her two nearest pursuers on the hop and opened up a healthy advantage before popping safely over the last and maintaining her lead all the way to the line to win by three lengths.

Following the race, her jockey said how well she'd been working at home and they were hopeful of a good result. Out of a black-type stayer on the Flat, Rhapsody In Blue, (1m 3f and German Listed-placed), herself a half-sister to the top-class Norse Dancer.

Purchased for £82,000 by Dan Astbury and Tim Talbot.

Emma Blue has all the right elements to earn some black type in bumpers this term before going over hurdles.

ERNEST GRAY
4YO BAY GELDING

TRAINER:	Alan King
PEDIGREE:	Walk In The Park – Emily Gray (Flemensfirth)
FORM (P2P NHF):	1 -
OPTIMUM TRIP:	2m +
GOING:	Good/Soft

⭐ **STAR POTENTIAL** ⭐

This well-bred gelding has already made his mark in a bumper and looks set to play his hand in some good races throughout the season.

Ernest Gray made his debut for Colin Bowe in a Punchestown point-to-point bumper for which he was sent off the 5/2 joint favourite.

Despite obvious signs of greenness, the gelding always travelled strongly towards the fore before moving into a share of the lead as the race developed over half a mile from home. Knuckling down in a taking manner and producing a good turn of foot, he looked the most likely winner before hanging on the run-in, causing him to drop to third.

Luckily with the rail to help him keep straight, he rallied deep inside the final furlong and stayed on strongly under hands and heels riding to regain the lead a few strides before the line to win by a neck.

Given his lack of maturity, there should be plenty of improvement to come. Colin Bowe said afterwards that he would've preferred for the gelding to start between the flags as he had schooled so well at home.

Ernest Gray is the first foal out of the smart race mare Emily Gray who won over hurdles over 2m-2m 5f including at Listed and Grade 3 level for Kim Bailey and Tim Hyde. His granddam was also a useful bumper performer and a 2m 4f hurdle winner, with the further family linking back to the smart staying hurdler Rose Ravine.

Purchased by Anthony Bromley of Highflyer Bloodstock for £105,000 and will now enter training with Alan King. Ernest Gray has obvious pace but as he develops and matures, I would expect him to prove most effective over staying distances. He has certainly inherited the toughness of his dam and could be quite exciting.

Ernest Gray – the first foal out of the Grade 3 winner Emily Gray (photo by Tattersalls)

EUREKA CREEK
5YO BAY MARE

TRAINER:	Emma Lavelle
PEDIGREE:	Jet Away – Copper River (Turgeon)
FORM:	1
OPTIMUM TRIP:	2m +
GOING:	Good to Soft

This Jet Away mare has joined Emma Lavelle after making a winning debut at Lisronagh in May.

Eureka Creek was one of only a few newcomers to line up in the 13-runner five-year-old mares' maiden but belied her inexperience by being ridden close to the pace before moving through to lead after the third from home despite, at times, jumping her fences a little scruffily.

Quickening in good style around the turn out of the back straight, she readily asserted her advantage and moved a few lengths clear of her nearest pursuer before taking the penultimate fence carefully. Still not asked for a full effort, she moved down to the last but slowed on the approach, allowing her stable companion, Mulberry Hill, to close on to her quarters before pulling out extra on the run to the line, crossing it with a length to spare with a further six lengths back to the third, Miss McGugen.

This only looked a modest affair with just five of the starting line-up managing to complete, but the form was bolstered by the third placing on her next two starts before scoring by 12 lengths in a maiden at Ballingarry. Mulberry Hill also confirmed the promise she showed by winning impressively on only her second start for Fergal O'Brien.

Eureka Creek looks a sturdy individual and should find suitable opportunities in races under Rules. Her dam is an unraced sister to the useful 2m-2m 4f hurdle/chase winner Tevere.

FINDTHETIME
5YO BAY GELDING

TRAINER:	Nicky Richards
PEDIGREE:	Shantou – Bisoguet (Definite Article)
FORM:	F -
OPTIMUM TRIP:	2m +
GOING:	Soft

Here is another useful-looking prospect to join Nicky Richards.

Findthetime was unlucky not to make a winning debut for Colin Bowe in a four-year-olds' maiden at Stradbally in December, when stalking the leading duo around the home bend before poking his nose to the front approaching the final fence, only to pitch on landing and crumple to the floor.

Overnight rain ensured ground conditions made that a real test of stamina for these younger horses, and as a result only two of the 11 starters managed to complete with Imperial Hope staying on dourly to regain the lead on the run-in to get the better of Planned Paradise by half a length. It's hard to suggest Findthetime would've won for sure, but he was the last off the bridle and hadn't been asked for a full effort at the time of his departure.

Despite the lack of finishers, the race received a form boost with the winner making a successful Rules debut for Oliver Sherwood in a bumper at

Doncaster, whilst the second showed promise for Neil Mulholland in a maiden hurdle at Worcester on only his second start under Rules.

This son of Shantou is a half-brother to the Paul Nicholls-trained Carry On The Magic, who finished second in a point but is yet to make an impact in two starts under Rules. His dam was placed over hurdles and fences in France and is a sister to the 2m 4f/2m 6f chase winner Doctor Pat.

Findthetime appears to possess natural pace to contest bumpers but I expect we'll see a true reflection of his ability when upped in trip to 2m 4f or further.

Nicky Richards – master of Greystoke (photo by Tattersalls)

FRONTIER GENERAL
4YO BAY GELDING

TRAINER:	TBC
PEDIGREE:	Mahler – Lady Zephyr (Toulon)
FORM:	1
OPTIMUM TRIP:	2m 4f +
GOING:	Soft

☆ **STAR POTENTIAL** ☆

Frontier General has both stamina and a turn of foot at his disposal.

Pat Doyle's son of Mahler was one of seven newcomers in the ten-strong line-up when making his debut in the pouring rain at Dromahane in May but displayed no signs of inexperience as he took to a share of the lead from the drop of the flag.

Setting a true tempo, the gelding was fleet of foot over most of his fences and maintained his two-length lead over the field at the fourth from home despite screwing in the air. Efficient over the next but knocked about on the landing side with the eventual runner-up going for a brave gap up his inside, Frontier General stood his ground and picked up well, jumping the penultimate fence with a length in hand before displaying a ready turn of foot on the sprint to the last.

Still hassled by Dream In The Park, both horses met the fence on a good stride but Frontier General's attitude was unwaning in the closing stages, digging deep and pulling out extra to eventually cross the line with a length and a half to spare over the gallant runner up.

Frontier General is a half-brother to three winners including Fergal O'Brien's Owen Na View (2m hurdle/useful chaser), Uptown Lady (2m 3f hurdle) and Gowithdflo (bumper). His dam, Lady Zephyr, was successful on seven occasions from 15 starts including three times both in bumpers and over hurdles (2m-2m 5f) for Nigel Twiston-Davies.

This individual looks above average. I would expect him to have the requisite pace for bumpers before progressing into a decent performer over hurdles and later fences. Distances in excess of 2m 4f on soft ground will likely suit in time.

FRONTLINE CITIZEN
5YO BAY GELDING

TRAINER:	TBC
PEDIGREE:	Sans Frontieres – Foreign Citizen (Presenting)
FORM:	1
OPTIMUM TRIP:	2m 4f +
GOING:	Soft

This home-bred gelding looks a slow burner.

Frontline Citizen made a pleasing start to his pointing career when staying on well to win a five-year-olds' maiden at Dawstown in May. The race had some substance to it with some of the ten runners having shown previous form, including Harley Dunne's runner-up who had previously finished third behind the talented Bareback Jack at Punchestown last February.

Frontline Citizen was one of the five newcomers in the line-up and was held up in the mid-division for the main part of the race before moving much closer at the third from home. Advancing into a share of second spot and still travelling kindly, he jumped to the front over the penultimate fence and showed a good attitude to knuckle down on the run to the last, where another bold leap propelled him up the run-in to hold Dancing With Deco by three lengths crossing the line, with a further four back to the staying-on Moore On Tour.

This was a likeable performance from Frontline Citizen which clocked a time eight seconds quicker than average.

Frontline Citizen is a half-brother to the 2m 5f hurdle winner Citizen Al and point winner/2m 4f hurdle winner Citizen's Army. He looks to possess a good deal of size so may take time to fully develop.

GAIA DU GOUET
5YO BAY MARE

TRAINER:	Dan Skelton
PEDIGREE:	Saddler Maker – Newhaven (Subotica)
FORM:	1 -
OPTIMUM TRIP:	2m
GOING:	Soft

A speedy daughter of Saddler Maker.

Gaia Du Gouet appeared to possess plenty of pace as she sprinted clear of Clearly Crazy on the run to the line to record a winning debut in the second division of the five-year-old mares' maiden at Tipperary in April for handler Paul Pierce.

Held up in the mid-division, she slowly crept closer to the pace on the final circuit and jumped into a share of the lead at the third from home before a bad mistake cost her momentum over the next. Asked to knuckle down and hold her advantage, the response was striking as she quickened in a matter of strides, putting daylight between herself and the second before pinging the last and scooting clear up the run-in to win by four lengths.

It only looked a modest contest and the time wasn't anything special, but the form has worked out well with both the third and fourth going on to win, whilst the second confirmed her ability with a good placed effort when last seen.

Gaia Du Gouet now resides at Dan Skelton's yard having been purchased for £85,000 at Cheltenham's April Sale.

A half-sister to the French 2m 1f-2m 2f chase winner Virtuose Du Gouet, her dam was successful in AQPS Flat races up to 1m 3f and later fences over 2m 3f and is a half-sister to the French 2m 5f-3m chase winner Mendiant.

This mare looks a strong but athletic model with plenty of speed. I expect her to go well in bumpers, should connections choose to start her there. She should also cope with softer ground given her round knee action.

Gaia Du Gouet – a strong daughter of Saddler Maker (photo by Tattersalls)

GANDHI MAKER
5YO BAY GELDING

TRAINER:	Philip Kirby
PEDIGREE:	Policy Maker – Thellya D'Arc (Assessor)
FORM:	1 -
OPTIMUM TRIP:	2m +
GOING:	Good to Soft

The field didn't see which way Gandhi Maker went when making all to win for Mary Doyle and Barry Stone at Tipperary in April.

The Policy Maker gelding was said to look exceptional in the paddock beforehand, and it wasn't long before he caught everyone's attention on the track as he took to the front when the tapes went up. Setting a good tempo, the bay jumped confidently and travelled smoothly, taking his two-length lead at the halfway point to five after jumping the third from home.

Continuing to bound along, Gandhi Maker seemed to relish the yielding underfoot conditions and effortlessly stretched his lead further off the home bend, jumping the final couple of fences perfectly before cruising up the run-in to record an eased-down six-length success.

This was a very taking debut and the form looks OK as the third, Chancycourt, beaten over 12 lengths, came out and finished within a length of Ted Hastings at Dromahane on his next start. Chancycourt is now in training with Fergal O'Brien and Ted Hastings is with Gordon Elliott.

Gandhi Maker is a second foal out of Thellya D'Arc who placed in chases over 2m 5f/2m 6f. She is a half-sister to the multiple 1m 4f-12.5f AQPS Flat and 2m 2f-2m 5f hurdle/chase winner Royal D'Arc and to the dam of the very smart Ball D'Arc.

An easy, fluid mover, Gandhi Maker will most likely be seen to best effect at tracks where he can stretch out and use his stride. He's also blessed with gears and could easily line up in a bumper before tackling hurdles. He's an exciting individual.

GENTLEMAN DE MAI
5YO BAY GELDING

TRAINER:	Rose Dobbin
PEDIGREE:	Saddler Maker – Ula De Mai (Passing Sale)
FORM:	2 -
OPTIMUM TRIP:	2m 4f +
GOING:	Soft/Heavy

Out of a half-sister to Bristol De Mai, this gelding has the potential to progress into a smart type under Rules.

Gentleman De Mai was forced to settle for the runner-up spot when making his debut at Ballindenisk for Denis Murphy and Jamie Codd last November, but the impression was that he'd bumped into a well-above-average type in Journey With Me and that feeling was later confirmed when he returned the impressive winner of the same Gowran Park bumper in which Bob Olinger made his successful debut 12 months previous.

Given a contrasting ride to Journey With Me, this son of Saddler Maker was held up throughout the contest and only started to make ground after the third from home. Moving into second spot approaching the penultimate fence, he stayed on strongly in the latter stages and although ultimately no match for the 12-length winner he was able to pull 18 lengths clear of the third.

Gentleman De Mai cost a small fortune when selling the way of Alan Harte Bloodstock for €110,000 as a store horse in June 2019 and since his pointing debut he's been sold privately to join Rose Dobbin's yard. He's an exciting horse to follow, both for this season and in those to come.

Like his three-parts brother, he'll be seen to best effect when encountering testing conditions.

GETAWAY LILY BEAR
5YO BAY MARE

TRAINER:	Olly Murphy
PEDIGREE:	Getaway – Jemima Jones (Flemensfirth)
FORM:	2 -
OPTIMUM TRIP:	2m +
GOING:	Good to Soft

This attractive mare is one to note in bumpers this term.

Getaway Lily Bear showed plenty of class on her debut in the four-year-old mares' maiden at Boulta in December when coming home in second place, three and a half lengths adrift of Aidan Fitzgerald's Queens River, who subsequently sold through the ring to Kieran McManus for £330,000 at Doncaster in December.

Always in the vanguard, Getaway Lily Bear jumped well for Eoin Mahon and tried to get away from the eventual winner after the second from home but was quickly put in her place once jumping the last despite staying on honestly to the line to draw eight lengths clear of Jillash in third.

Out of an unraced half-sister to the sadly ill-fated useful hurdle/chase winner (2m-2m 4f) Theo from the family of the bumper/useful 2m 4f hurdle winner Leinster.

Getaway Lily Bear has a touch of quality and should be found winning opportunities in the colours of Owners Group having been purchased by Highflyer Bloodstock for £75,000 at the same sale where her conqueror was sold.

She handled the testing conditions well on her debut but Getaway's progeny tend to prefer a better surface.

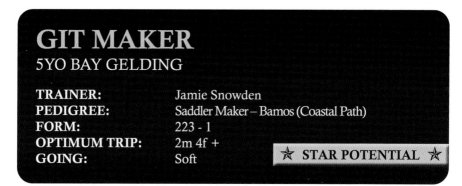

GIT MAKER
5YO BAY GELDING

TRAINER:	Jamie Snowden
PEDIGREE:	Saddler Maker – Bamos (Coastal Path)
FORM:	223 - 1
OPTIMUM TRIP:	2m 4f +
GOING:	Soft

★ STAR POTENTIAL ★

This promising son of Saddler Maker chased home the now 131-rated Up For Parol and had a subsequent eight-length point winner a head back in third on his debut at Damma House last November. He then filled the same spot a fortnight later, this time at Loughbrickland where he tried to make most of the running in a race won by Ballyhawkish who was subsequently bought by Neil King for £88,000.

Third next time at Tattersalls Farm behind Gold Cup Bailly – a horse who managed to get within four lengths of the subsequent Grade 1 winner Ahoy Senor in a maiden hurdle at Ayr. Git Maker finally gained his deserved success at Necarne in May when cruising home to record an easy ten-length success over the newcomer Hymac, controlling matters from the drop of the flag.

Git Maker looks a classy and tough recruit who ought to do well for Jamie Snowden, who was standing alongside Tom Malone when the hammer came down at the Goffs UK Spring Sale to the tune of £105,000.

He's the first foal out of an unraced half-sister to a useful French/Italian 2m 1f-2m 5f hurdle/chase winner. He looks a stayer but also shows natural pace. He could be above average.

GIVEGA
5YO BAY GELDING

TRAINER:	Gary Moore
PEDIGREE:	Authorized – Sivega (Robin Des Champs)
FORM:	1
OPTIMUM TRIP:	2m +
GOING:	Soft

☆ **STAR POTENTIAL** ☆

Givega gave one of the most visually impressive performances of the truncated season when coming home in front under a motionless Barry O'Neill at Tralee in late May and could quite simply be anything.

The Authorized gelding was one of several newcomers in the 13-strong line-up for the five-year-olds' maiden but proved lack of experience to be no factor when bounding to the front with over a circuit to travel. Jumping well, he oozed class as he continued to pour on the pressure over the final couple of fences and cruised clear up the run-in after another spring-heeled leap at the last, crossing the line with considerably more in hand than the two-length winning margin would suggest.

Not only did this look a serious performance, but the clock recorded a time 12 seconds faster than standard. That's only four seconds slower than the four-year-olds' maiden where the pace was contested from the outset.

Givega not only looked plucked from the top drawer on track, but he also boasts a top-class pedigree being out of a half-sister to the outstanding hurdler, Quevega. His half-brother is also a Listed winner over hurdles (2m 2f) and his dam won an AQPS Flat race over 1m 4f.

Interestingly, he now resides at Gary Moore's yard after being bought privately. Surely, he'll take in some nice races this season, presumably over hurdles, and it wouldn't be a surprise to see him around Sandown at some point. He could even be a Festival sort of horse.

GLOBAL ASSEMBLY
4YO BAY GELDING

TRAINER:	TBC
PEDIGREE:	Kayf Tara – Anadama (Anshan)
FORM:	3 -
OPTIMUM TRIP:	2m 4f +
GOING:	Soft/Heavy

Global Assembly looks like the type that will flourish when he encounters some winter ground.

The Kayf Tara gelding made his debut in a strongly contested six-runner four-year-old geldings' maiden at Fairyhouse in April – a race won by Harry Des Ongrais who beat Watch House Cross by ten lengths, with that runner-up since franking the form by winning his next start by five lengths.

Global Assembly finished third, a further ten lengths behind Watch House Cross, but he looked most unsuited to the good to yielding conditions and it's to his great credit that he was not only able to stay with the front pair for so long, but to finish in the manner in which he did.

Given Tom Keating's horses always tend to come on for their debuts, I'm sure we'll see an improved performance next time, especially if there's plenty of give in the ground. With that in mind, connections may try and win a point with him this autumn before heading to the sales, or he may have already been sold privately.

By Kayf Tara out of an Anshan mare who placed in points and over hurdles and is a half-sister to the bumper/2m-3m hurdle winner Stadium Project out of an unraced half-sister to the prolific 2m-3m 1f chase winner Pinemartin.

Global Assembly already fills the eye but has plenty of room for more physical development. He could slip under the radar when he pops up under Rules. Soft ground and a trip in excess of 2m 4f will bring out the best in him.

GUILY BILLY
5YO GREY GELDING

TRAINER:	Henry de Bromhead
PEDIGREE:	Coastal Path – Ukie (Dom Alco)
FORM:	P/1 -
OPTIMUM TRIP:	2m 4f +
GOING:	Soft

★ STAR POTENTIAL ★

Expectations will be high for this gorgeous grey as he makes his Rules debut for Cheveley Park Stud having passed through the sales ring for £310,000.

Guily Billy was disappointingly pulled up with two fences to jump on his debut at Borris House in March 2020 when sent off the 2/1 favourite, but clearly benefited for the time away from the track when winning impressively on his reappearance at Tinahely last November.

Conditions were dismal but the son of Coastal Path went to the front from the drop of the flag and never looked back, demonstrating both a clean round of jumping and an abundance of stamina as he pulled away from his nearest pursuer on the uphill climb to the second from home. Not for stopping, he cleared the remaining fences in good style and crossed the line strongly with four lengths in hand over Captain Quint with a further 15 lengths back to the third.

Captain Quint has since sold to Gerry Hogan acting on behalf of Rose Dobbin for £110,000, whilst Hello Judge, who was pulled up before the penultimate fence, subsequently won on his hurdling debut for Ann Hamilton having been purchased in a private deal from Colin Bowe.

By Coastal Path out of a French 2m 1f hurdle winner who is a half-sister to Jimmy Moffatt's 2m 4f hurdle winner Quel Elite.

Guily Billy was entered to make his debut for Henry de Bromhead in the spring but is obviously taking a while to come to hand. Ultimately, he looks a dour stayer on winter ground, and we probably won't see his true ability until he tackles fences in seasons to come.

Guily Billy – a gorgeous grey due to run in the colours of Cheveley Park Stud (photo by Tattersalls)

HAPPY D'EX
4YO GREY GELDING

TRAINER:	Gordon Elliott
PEDIGREE:	Saddler Maker – Soiree D'Ex (Fragrant Mix)
FORM:	1
OPTIMUM TRIP:	2m +
GOING:	Soft

Only three runners went to post for the four-year-old mares' maiden at Dromahane in early May but Happy D'Ex had far too much class and came home the very easy 15-length winner.

Watching on from the rear and allowing the others to pave the way, Happy D'Ex travelled comfortably on the bridle before making a deliberate challenge around the turn out of the back straight where she moved up to the leader's quarters. Clearly going best, she moved to the front with the minimal amount of fuss after jumping the third from home and quickly pulled clear of her toiling opposition over the final couple of fences, eventually crossing the line with any amount in hand.

This may not have been a competitive affair, but Harry's Hottie who finished second had shown a fair level of ability on her debut when finishing second to Jenny Flex and the third has since filled the same position behind Emma Blue at Ballingarry.

Happy D'Ex looks to have plenty of speed. Her dam is a 11.5f-1m 5f AQPS Flat winner and is a half-sister to a French-Listed placed 2m 5f-2m 7f chase winner.

Purchased for £195,000 at the Goffs Spring Sale at Doncaster in May, I imagine we'll be seeing this speedy filly in a bumper before she goes over hurdles next season.

HARRY DES ONGRAIS
4YO GREY GELDING

TRAINER:	TBC
PEDIGREE:	Crillon – Lola Des Ongrais (Myrakalu)
FORM:	1 -
OPTIMUM TRIP:	2m +
GOING:	Soft

Here is a gelding that should have improved for a summer at grass.

Harry Des Ongrais still had plenty of frame to fill when making his debut in the four-year-old geldings' maiden at Fairyhouse in April but showed his superior class to come home the ten-length easy winner of the six-runner contest in the famous colours of Milestone Bloodstock Ltd for Colin Bowe.

Despite the small field, this was a truly run race and Harry Des Ongrais always travelled strongly in his comfort zone before moving through to challenge for the lead with a quick leap over the fifth from home. From there he shared the running with Watch House Cross but continually outjumped that horse before quickening into the home bend and entering the straight with a widening advantage, which he continued to extend all the way to the line despite an awkward leap at the last.

This was a taking performance by the good-looking grey and not only was the time 11 seconds quicker than standard, but the form received a significant boost when the second bolted up next time at Dromahane – a race which looked above average and the third has since won.

A half-brother to French winners Dino Des Ongrais (2m 1f/2m 4f chase) and Viking Des Ongrais (2m 4f hurdle). His dam is a 1m 3f-14.5f AQPS Flat winner from the family of the smart 2m-2m 4f chaser Manhattan Castle.

Harry Des Ongrais was purchased by Henry de Bromhead as a store horse for €60,000 and could well enter training with him this season. He's very much a horse blessed with speed but, given the room for physical development, he has the potential to develop into a useful prospect over a range of trips.

HARVIE WALLBANGER
5YO BAY GELDING

TRAINER:	John O'Shea
PEDIGREE:	Mahler – Initforthecrack (Morozov)
FORM:	1 -
OPTIMUM TRIP:	2m 4f +
GOING:	Good

Harvie Wallbanger looks a lovely long-term prospect.

The son of Mahler made a winning debut in a hotly contested 15-runner five-year-old geldings' maiden at Cork in April, coming home the wide margin winner after his only realistic challenger fell when narrowly headed at the second from home.

Harvie Wallbanger had always travelled strongly up with the pace under Chris O'Donovan and moved through to challenge for the lead after the fourth from home. Knuckling down well and finding plenty for pressure, he still had a little to do when left in the lead with a commanding advantage but there was plenty to like about the way he kept on to the line thereafter despite an untidy leap at the last.

It would've been interesting to see how he fared had he been forced to battle to the line but even without a true test, he's emerged as a promising individual with the form holding up well due to the second being beaten only three parts of a length on his next start. The sixth has also subsequently finished second.

Harvie Wallbanger is a sizable individual and had been working well at home prior to his debut with his previous handler stating, "He's a lovely horse that has improved in his work at home for a bit of nice ground … he's a beautiful mover."

Out of an unraced half-sister to a bumper/2m 6f hurdle winner. His further family ties in with the useful 2m 5f-3m hurdle/chase winner Wild Crack – the dam of Cue Card.

Harvie Wallbanger may need time to thrive, but he boasts a useful pedigree and may be primed for a spring campaign given his preference for nicer ground.

HEREWEGOHONEY
5YO BAY MARE

TRAINER:	Fergal O'Brien
PEDIGREE:	Sageburg – Knappogue Honey (Anshan)
FORM:	1
OPTIMUM TRIP:	2m +
GOING:	Soft

Herewegohoney will carry the colours of Midland Park Racing.

The classy-looking daughter of Sageburg made a lasting impression when coming clear in the hands of Eoin Mahon to win on her debut at Necarne in May for handler Paurick O'Connor.

Patiently ridden in the testing conditions, Herewegohoney was keen in the early stages but made ground effortlessly as the race progressed and moved into a prominent position after the third from home. Touching down in front over the next, she quickly put distance between herself and the field and although making an untidy shape over the last and pecking on landing, she had plenty left in the tank to pull clear up the hill and cross the line by a commanding four lengths from Harbour Queen with the subsequent winner, Getalady, three lengths back in third.

Not only has the form of that race worked out well, but it also clocked a time two seconds above standard, seven seconds quicker than the four-year-old mares' maiden and only ten seconds behind the five-year-old geldings' maiden on the same card.

Herewegohoney has plenty of size and comes from a lovely family. She is a half-sister to the ultra-tough ten-time winner Man Of Steel (bumper/2m 4f-3m 3f hurdle/chase), Getaway Honey (point/bumper) and Who You For (point/bumper).

Purchased by current connections at Cheltenham's May Sale, she could look well bought for £62,000. The pace she showed when making up ground bodes well for bumpers before progressing through the ranks.

HOLLY HARTINGO
5YO BAY MARE

TRAINER:	Alastair Ralph
PEDIGREE:	Well Chosen – Hazel Toi (Mister Lord)
FORM:	6 - 2
OPTIMUM TRIP:	2m +
GOING:	Good to Soft

Holly Hartingo may not boast a strong pedigree, but she has shown enough to suggest success under Rules awaits.

The Well Chosen mare finished a modest sixth on her debut at Cork's pointing track in April, travelling nicely in a prominent position in the early stages before losing her pitch on the final circuit and finishing at the one pace some 17 lengths behind the winner, First Glance.

Benefiting for that experience, she then went to Dromahane in early May and finished a close second, only beaten three parts of a length behind the newcomer, Sharp Shadow. Again, always prominent and although a little sketchy over her fences, she stuck on gamely at the one pace and pulled six lengths clear of the third.

Holly Hartingo is a nice mare to look at. She's a good size, moves well and has a willing attitude. She looks capable of success under Rules, maybe once handicapping, and could prove a good buy for £27,000.

Given she's by Well Chosen out of a Mister Lord mare – both profound influences of stamina – she'll be best when tackling a trip.

HOW WILL I KNOW
4YO BAY GELDING

TRAINER:	Harry Fry
PEDIGREE:	Ocovango – Balleen Rose (Old Vic)
FORM (P2P NHF):	2 -
OPTIMUM TRIP:	2m +
GOING:	Soft

It's only a matter of time before the Ocovango gelding gets off the mark.

David Fitzgerald's How Will I Know emerged with great credit when finishing second, beaten only a neck, by the rallying Ernest Gray in a point-to-point bumper at Punchestown in March. Sent off an unfancied 20/1 shot, the gelding travelled powerfully at the rear of the field for most of the extended 2m contest before making eye-catching progress when demonstrating a good burst of speed to cut through the pack over half a mile from home.

Continuing his forward movement as the tempo increased, How Will I Know knuckled down well to pick up the running passing the furlong pole only to be headed by a resurgent Ernest Gray a few strides before the line.

This was a good effort from the four-year-old, and although the form has not worked out well, he showed he has both pace and a good attitude which will stand him in good stead for racing under Rules.

How Will I Know is a half-brother to the Keith Dalgleish-trained Murphy's Law who won a hurdle/chase over 2m 4f-2m 7f, and also Emma Lavelle's Old Rascals who won over hurdles (2m 5f). His dam placed in bumpers and is a half-sister to the five-time winner over 2m-2m 3f hurdle/chase, Fireball Macnamara.

Given the stamina on the bottom line of How Will I Know's pedigree, he ought to get a trip in time, but the Ocovango side adds speed. Soft ground could be important to him.

HURLERONTHEDITCH
5YO CHESTNUT GELDING

TRAINER:	Kim Bailey
PEDIGREE:	Shirocco – Maid Of Malabar (Oscar Schindler)
FORM:	U -
FORM (P2P NHF):	1 -
OPTIMUM TRIP:	2m +
GOING:	Soft

We didn't see much of Michael Kennedy's Hurlerontheditch on his pointing debut at Boulta last November as he unseated at the sixth fence, but there was plenty to like about his gritty victory in a 2m 2f point-to-point bumper at Wexford in March.

Held up for a good chunk of the race, the Shirocco gelding weaved his way through the field over half a mile from home, moving into contention going easily around the turn into the straight before challenging widest of all. Asked for an effort with over a furlong to travel, he knuckled down gamely and found an extra gear in the closing stages to reel in the leader before eventually crossing the line with one-and-three-quarter lengths to spare over the favourite, Chrissies Diamond, with the same distance back to Patricks Hill.

That form looks OK with the third subsequently narrowly beaten over hurdles whilst the seventh looked the likely winner of a point-to-point at Fairyhouse on his next start only to unseat at the last.

Hurlerontheditch is a brother to the bumper/2m 4f hurdle winner Majestic Maid whilst his dam also won a bumper before finding success over fences. She is a half-sister to a 2m-2m 4f hurdle winner out of an unraced half-sister to 3m-3m 1f hurdle winner Knighton Lad.

Purchased by Aiden Murphy acting on behalf of Kim Bailey for £85,000, there's plenty to like about this gelding, not least his battling qualities but also the fine blend of speed and stamina. His smooth travelling will stand him in good stead for racing under Rules.

Hurlerontheditch – battled bravely to success in a point-to-point bumper (photo by Tattersalls)

INGENIOUS STROKE
5YO BAY GELDING

TRAINER:	Henry de Bromhead
PEDIGREE:	Jet Away – Just For Jean (Presenting)
FORM:	61 -
OPTIMUM TRIP:	2m +
GOING:	Good to Soft

Ingenious Stroke has the pace to make an impact in bumpers or the two-mile hurdle division in his first season under Rules.

The attractive son of Jet Away never threatened to get involved on his debut in a hotly contested four-year-olds' maiden at Ballycrystal last October, always towards the rear and only making modest headway over the final couple of fences to finish just shy of seven lengths behind Tamgho Borget who fought out a finish with Unanswered Prayers, both now with Paul Nicholls and Chris Gordon respectively.

Ingenious Stroke wasn't seen again until April but made a tidy return when making every yard at Cork in an incident-packed five-year-old geldings' maiden, staying on bravely over the final few fences to fend off a late challenge from Loughderg Rocco by three parts of a length with 12 lengths back to the third, Cosmic Outlaw.

That form couldn't have worked out better with the runner-up subsequently winning in a good time at Fairyhouse just over a fortnight later, whilst the third also won next time out at Tipperary.

Clearly, the Jet Away gelding has a decent engine and whilst he doesn't make too many mistakes at his fences, he can be too careful and waste time in the air. With time his confidence should grow, and in turn further improvement can be expected.

A half-brother to the 2m 4f chase winner Fit For Fifty, his dam was a bumper/2m 1f hurdle winner and is a half-sister to the bumper/2m-3m hurdle/ useful chase winner World Wide Web from the family of Irish National winner Sweet Dreams.

Despite the obvious stamina in Ingenious Stroke's pedigree, I fully expect him to make use of his natural pace this season.

ITSALLINTHECLOUDS
5YO BAY GELDING

TRAINER:	TBC
PEDIGREE:	Cloudings – Carrie Bradshaw (Accordion)
FORM:	1 -
OPTIMUM TRIP:	2m 4f +
GOING:	Soft

This physically imposing gelding could slip under the radar when he appears under Rules.

Itsallintheclouds made a real impression when embarking on his debut in an extended 3m 1f maiden at Aldington in April for Tom Ellis and Gina Andrews. Happy to sit behind the pace as the leader went a good gallop, the grey (officially listed as bay) travelled powerfully and jumped professionally before making stealthy headway to close on the pace-setter inside the final half-mile.

Travelling wide and catching the eye, Gina Andrews timed her run to perfection as she allowed her mount to jump to the front over the second from home before asking him to knuckle down off the home turn. Responding generously, the grey asserted and quickly took a couple of lengths out of his nearest pursuer before jumping the last fluently to come clear up the run-in to win by a widening five lengths in a fast time.

This was a very taking debut from the debutant five-year-old and the form has worked out extremely well with the second, third and fourth all winning since.

Itsallintheclouds, who hails from the family of Gunner Welburn, was due to be sold at Cheltenham's April Sale but was withdrawn, presumably due to him being picked up in a private deal.

Wherever he starts, he's an exciting recruit and one to very much keep onside. Undoubtedly, he'll be best suited to some soft ground and a trip which brings his stamina into play. He could be above average.

Itsallintheclouds – could slip under the radar (photo by Craig Payne)

JENNY FLEX
4YO BAY FILLY

TRAINER:	TBC
PEDIGREE:	Walk In The Park – Dark Mimosa (Bahri)
FORM:	21 -
OPTIMUM TRIP:	2m +
GOING:	Soft

A physically imposing daughter of Walk In The Park and a half-sister to Scarlet And Dove out of Dark Mimosa – a half-sister to the late Our Conor.

Jenny Flex passed through the ring as a foal for €22,000 back in 2017 and was later sold as a store horse in August 2020 for €75,000 to Mags O'Toole before making her debut in a fillies' point-to-point bumper at Punchestown in March for Colin Bowe and Brian Acheson. There she finished second, beaten nine and a half lengths by J P McManus' Limerick Lace, attempting to make all, only to be headed inside the final furlong but keeping on at the one pace to stay over seven lengths clear of the third.

Jenny Flex returned the following month in a point-to-point at Cork and looked a class above her opposition as she travelled strongly up with the pace before moving into a clear advantage before the fifth from home. Continuing to cruise on the bridle despite several flashes of the tail, she had the race in full control as she pulled away after the last, where her nearest pursuer fell, leaving her to come home ten lengths clear of her stable companion Harry's Hottie.

Jenny Flex has already shown herself to have plenty of natural ability and given time she has the potential to develop into a top-class prospect. With a pedigree littered with speed but also a hint of stamina, she could be versatile with regards to trip. She's a very exciting filly to follow this season and beyond.

JET OF MAGIC
5YO BAY GELDING

TRAINER:	Oliver Greenall
PEDIGREE:	Jet Away – Ginandit (Definite Article)
FORM (P2P NHF):	1 -
OPTIMUM TRIP:	2m +
GOING:	Good to Soft

This scopey son of Jet Away has the potential to develop into a nice prospect for Oliver Greenall.

Jet Of Magic was another of Denis Murphy's string to be all dressed up with nowhere to race in the point-to-point division, so took advantage of a point-to-point bumper at Punchestown in March where he was sent off at odds of 100/30 under Jamie Codd.

Patiently ridden, the pair raced in the rear of mid-division for a good chunk of the 2m 4f contest before making progress on the wide outside of the field to move on to the heels of the leading pack inside the final mile. Still travelling well as the pace increased over two furlongs from home, the gelding found the extra gear needed entering the straight and quickly moved through to lead with a furlong to go before finding plenty for pressure to pull away in the closing stages and win by four lengths from Golas Tiep.

This was a classy performance from the five-year-old and although the form hasn't worked out very well, he looks the type who should do better. That said, he's the seventh foal out of Ginandit and only Dara's Present managed to win a point-to-point before showing very little for Harry Whittington.

Dan Astbury and Timothy Talbot parted with £75,000 at Cheltenham's March Sale and he will now enter training with Oliver Greenall.

Given he's already won over 2m 4f, he could stay at that trip but he has natural pace and could cope with a drop back to 2m. There should be some winning opportunities for him over hurdles.

JIM KEY
5YO BAY GELDING

TRAINER:	TBC
PEDIGREE:	Shantou – Queeny's Princess (Daggers Drawn)
FORM:	1 -
OPTIMUM TRIP:	2m
GOING:	Soft

☆ **STAR POTENTIAL** ☆

Jim Key looks a perfect candidate for the two-mile hurdle division.

John Staunton's gelding created a lasting impression on his debut in a decent standard four-year-old geldings' maiden at Lisronagh last November where he received a confident ride from Derek O'Connor. Held on to for much of the race, it was only approaching the second from home that the son of Shantou was asked for any sort of effort, and the response was impressive, quickening in a matter of strides with a sweeping run around the outside of the field to move into a challenging position.

Despite a less than fluent leap over the penultimate fence, none of the field could live with the extraordinary burst of speed that Jim Key produced as he quickly moved to the lead on the run to the last. Jumping that fence safely, he continued to power clear on the run to the line, eventually coming home ten lengths to the good over Brorson, who in turn was three lengths clear of the third.

Not only was this a visually impressive display, but it was also good on the clock which recorded a time 13 seconds quicker than standard and six seconds faster than the second division of the maiden. Derek O'Connor also had a job bringing the gelding to a stop once he had crossed the line.

Sold at the Goffs UK Sale in November, he was second only to Jonbon on the top-lot list as Hamish Macauley parted with £215,000 on behalf of a new client.

Jim Key has a pedigree very much biased towards speed being a half-brother to the all-weather 1m winner Tagalaka out of a half-sister to the useful 1m winner Princess Genista, who also stayed 2m and is the dam of the very smart Give Notice and Times Up.

Not the biggest in stature, Jim Key looks a proper hurdling type and ought to be best suited to two miles. He's exciting.

KING ARISE
4YO GREY GELDING

TRAINER:	Dr Richard Newland
PEDIGREE:	Kingston Hill – Aries Ballerina (Peintre Celebre)
FORM (P2P NHF):	1 -
OPTIMUM TRIP:	2m
GOING:	Good to Soft

Worcestershire-based Tom Weston likes to buy foals and produce them to win in the point-to-point sphere before selling them again, and he looks to have executed that perfectly here with King Arise.

The striking grey made his debut under the guidance of Luke Scott in the two-mile point-to-point bumper at Garthorpe in April. Always travelling strongly in the mid-division for the majority of the race, it wasn't until inside the final half-mile that the son of Kingston Hill started to move closer to the pace, switching inside the leader, Universal Run, before demonstrating a useful turn of foot to quicken clear inside the final furlong to win by an easy five lengths.

King Arise is a useful-looking model that has a nice way of travelling through a race and since his success he has been picked up in a private deal by Foxtrot Racing. He will now enter training with Dr Richard Newland.

Out of an unraced half-sister to the 1m 2f winner Toy Show and 6f-7f winner West Leake Hare from the family of the smart miler Inglenook.

King Arise looks the ideal type for an autumn bumper before a spring campaign over hurdles. Given his sire loved a bit of give underfoot, King Arise may also cope well with winter ground.

KNOWSLEY ROAD
4YO BAY GELDING

TRAINER:	Paul Nicholls
PEDIGREE:	Flemensfirth – Rowanville Lady (Milan)
FORM:	2
OPTIMUM TRIP:	2m +
GOING:	Soft

This son of Flemensfirth is an embryonic chaser and did well to show so much first time out.

Knowsley Road made his debut in an above-average four-year-old geldings' maiden at Tralee in May – a race which clocked a time 16 seconds quicker than average and 34 seconds faster than the four-year-old mares' maiden half an hour earlier.

Always on the pace, this gelding travelled like a classy horse and put in several good leaps over his fences before laying down a strong challenge for the lead off the home turn. Slightly sticky on landing over the penultimate fence, he took a few strides and signals of encouragement from the saddle to pick up but was in top flight by the time he'd reached the last. There he cleared the fence in great style and looked for all the winner as he moved away with momentum, poking his nose to the front and sticking his neck out all the way to the line, only to be overtaken in the shadows of the post by the confidently ridden City Chief.

That horse has since passed through the ring at Cheltenham's May Sale for £210,000, selling the way of Highflyer Bloodstock acting on behalf of Nicky Henderson. This gelding sold at the same sale and fetched £135,000 with the final bid going to Tom Malone standing alongside Paul Nicholls.

Out of a half-sister to the useful 2m 4f-4m chase winner Jovial Joey from the family of the high-class bumper/2m hurdle winner Joe Mac and high-class 2m-2m 4f chaser Direct Route.

This is the type of horse Paul Nicholls does very well with. He's only going to progress as he matures and fills his frame.

LAST QUARTER
4YO BAY GELDING

TRAINER:	David Pipe
PEDIGREE:	Walk In The Park – Lunar Path (Night Shift)
FORM (P2P NHF):	1 -
OPTIMUM TRIP:	2m +
GOING:	Soft

☆ **STAR POTENTIAL** ☆

Last Quarter looks like a very useful prospect and can make his presence felt over hurdles this term.

The Walk In The Park gelding made a winning racecourse debut for Colin Bowe in a 2m 4f point-to-point bumper at Punchestown back in March in the hands of Barry O'Neill. Sent off the 7/4 favourite and keen to get on with things, Last Quarter soon made his way to the front and set a steady pace before increasing the tempo inside the last half-mile.

Caught a little flat-footed when the eventual runner-up quickened off the bend for home, Last Quarter knuckled down determinedly, demonstrating both a very likeable attitude and plenty of stamina reserves to readily regain the lead on the run-in before crossing the line with a little more in hand than the one-and-a-half-length winning margin would suggest.

From a family littered with speed and stamina. Both his half-brothers, Represented and Cedar Valley, won bumpers, whilst his dam was a winner over 1m 1f on the Flat before winning a Listed hurdle over 2m 2f. She is a half-sister to Sonevafushi, a useful hurdler/chaser who stayed 3m 3f, and also Celtic Son who stayed 3m 1f.

Last Quarter looks above average and should be followed closely for David Pipe.

LOUGHDERG ROCCO
5YO BROWN GELDING

TRAINER:	Laura Morgan
PEDIGREE:	Shirocco – Banaltra (Definite Article)
FORM:	2 - 1
OPTIMUM TRIP:	2m 4f +
GOING:	Good to Soft

Laura Morgan does exceptionally well with her smaller string of horses and Loughderg Rocco looks another great addition to the team.

The Denis Murphy-trained gelding went down fighting by three parts of a length on his debut at Cork in April, staying on well over the final couple of fences and strongly pressing the winner on the run-in only for the line to come in time. That form received a boost when the third – beaten 12 lengths by Loughderg Rocco – came out and won next time and now enters training with Rose Dobbin.

Benefiting from that run, this Shirocco gelding then went to Fairyhouse just over a fortnight later where he came home the easy 12-length winner from the experienced Tim Pat with a further two lengths back to the third. On that occasion he moved to the front with a good leap over the penultimate fence before asserting around the home bend to come clear over the last and power through the line to clock a good time.

A half-brother to a bumper winner out of an unraced half-sister to the 2m 4f-2m 5f hurdle/chase winner Old Brigade from the family of the smart jumper Quazar.

Purchased for £75,000 at the Goffs UK Spring Sale at Doncaster in May, this gelding looks a real galloper with a touch of class. I'm sure his trainer will place him to great effect and success in his first season under Rules can be expected.

He could be best suited to good ground.

MARVEL DE CERISY
4YO CHESTNUT GELDING

TRAINER:	Pat Doyle
PEDIGREE:	Masked Marvel – Midalisy (Medaaly)
FORM:	1 -
OPTIMUM TRIP:	2m +
GOING:	Good to Soft

★ STAR POTENTIAL ★

This chestnut gelding has the world at his feet.

Marvel De Cerisy scorched the turf from the drop of the flag on his debut in a four-year-old geldings' maiden at Tipperary in April. Trained by Pat Doyle and ridden by Pa King, the gelding set a strong tempo throughout, bouncing off the good to yielding ground and attacking his fences with confidence. Not even a serious peck on landing after the fourth from home could interrupt the gelding's momentum as he quickly regathered his stride and continued to maintain his lead.

Sailing over the next, he then effortlessly pulled further clear on the turn into the straight before winging the penultimate fence and demonstrating an impressive turn of foot on the run to the last. One final foot-assured leap there left the race in no doubt as he powered clear up the run-in to record a five-length success over A Different Kind with a length back to The Goffer in third.

This was a seriously impressive debut from the four-year-old, not only from a visual aspect but the time was also nine seconds quicker than standard – the quickest by some margin on the day. Pat Doyle said after the race, "He'd never been outside our front gate until today so we think he'll improve from that. He should have a good future on the track now."

Marvel De Cerisy is a half-brother to the useful seven-time French 2m 1f-2m 3f hurdle/chase winner Vangel De Cerisy and also Michael Scudamore's bumper/2m hurdle winner Thor De Cerisy.

Whether he stays with Pat Doyle or ends up in one of the top Irish yards remains to be seen, but wherever he ends up, he's a serious horse and must be given the utmost of respect.

MELK ABBEY
5YO BAY MARE

TRAINER:	Henry de Bromhead
PEDIGREE:	Sholokhov – Carrig'n May (Classic Cliche)
FORM:	3 - 1
OPTIMUM TRIP:	2m 4f +
GOING:	Soft

This home-bred mare comes from a useful family and is one to watch for as she enters training with Henry de Bromhead.

Melk Abbey showed plenty of potential when filling third spot on her pointing debut at Cork back in April and clearly benefited for that experience when getting off the mark in fine style at Dromahane in May.

That was only a modest affair in which the pace was sedate from the outset but, having tracked the leaders for the first half of the race, Melk Abbey moved through to lead with over a circuit to go and came clear with two fences to jump, eventually crossing the line with five lengths in hand over Pegs Theatre with a further 15 lengths back to the third, Knockanora Lady.

In winning, she beat a 12-runner field, most of which went into the race with more experience than her, and although the time was slow due to the slow tempo, she emerged as a smart-looking prospect and it's interesting that connections have chosen to send her to Henry de Bromhead – a dab hand with the mares.

Melk Abbey is the second foal out of Carrig'n May, a point winner who placed in bumpers and won a maiden hurdle for Michael Winter. She is a half-sister to the bumper and useful 2m3f-3f hurdle/chase winner Creepy and bumper/2m1f chase winner Dinny Lacey.

Bought by Noel Fehily of Hagg Hill Farm for £65,000 at the Cheltenham May Sale, she may prove best when the emphasis is on stamina.

MR FRED ROGERS
5YO BAY GELDING

TRAINER:	TBC
PEDIGREE:	Sholokhov – Play The Wing (Bob Back)
FORM:	1 -
OPTIMUM TRIP:	2m 4f +
GOING:	Good to Soft

This looks an above-average type.

Mr Fred Rogers made a tidy winning debut in a point-to-point bumper at Tipperary in March for William Murphy and Pa King. On paper it looked a strong 13-runner contest with Henry de Bromhead and Denise Foster both represented but it was this gelding, who was tongue-tied, that showed the better turn of foot inside the final furlong to cross the line with just shy of two lengths to spare over Gortmillish with another promising type in Contemplatemyfaith a head back in third.

Mr Fred Rogers was ridden patiently towards the rear for a good chunk of the extended 2m 3f contest but made eye-catching progress on the outside over half a mile from home and moved into a challenging position still travelling well inside the final three furlongs. Once ridden, the gelding quickly responded and poked his nose to the front with a good burst of speed before maintaining his strong run to the line.

Mr Fred Rogers is the second foal out of Play The Wing, who was unsuccessful in races but is a half-sister to the 2m4f/3m hurdle winner Supreme Huntress. She was out of an unraced half-sister to the useful 2m-2m4f jumper Chevalier Errant.

Unsold for £115,000, I'm unsure of Mr Fred Rogers' whereabouts but he looks a nice type for racing under Rules. Two and a half miles on decent ground ought to see the gelding in the best light.

NIGHT DUTY
5YO BROWN GELDING

TRAINER:	Fergal O'Brien
PEDIGREE:	Kalanisi – Lerichi (Shardari)
FORM:	1
OPTIMUM TRIP:	2m +
GOING:	Soft

A very easy winner of an English point-to-point.

Night Duty could have been called the winner a long way from home on his debut at Kingston Blount, Oxfordshire, in May where he won division one of the three-mile maiden by a very easy 18 lengths for trainer Francesca Nimmo in the hands of the Aintree Foxhunters' Chase-winning jockey James King.

Never far from the pace, the good-looking gelding eventually moved to the front from the halfway point and the field simply couldn't go with him. Jumping with confidence and producing some fantastic leaps, notably over the third from home, he really poured on the pressure and extended clear down the home straight before slowing right down approaching the last, which he popped over nicely to canter clear up the run-in to win as he liked.

Sent to the Goffs UK Spring Sale at Doncaster, he fetched £65,000 and is now in the care of Fergal O'Brien.

A half-brother to point/2m 4f and 2m 5f hurdle winner King Calvin, 2m 2f hurdle/2m 3f chase winner Prince Of Denial from the family of the very useful Hey Big Spender and Midlands National winner Miss Orchestra (dam of Value At Risk and Battlecry).

This well-bred gelding will likely start in a bumper, but ultimately he looks like a proper chaser for further down the line. He should prove versatile over a range of trips.

Night Duty – another exciting recruit to join Fergal O'Brien (photo by Neale Blackburn)

PAUDIE
5YO BAY GELDING

TRAINER:	Max Young
PEDIGREE:	Fame And Glory – Honeyed (Persian Mews)
FORM:	P - 2
OPTIMUM TRIP:	2m +
GOING:	Soft

Paudie didn't show a great deal when pulled up before the third from home on his debut at Tipperary in April but demonstrated far more next time when staying on well to finish a solid second to Dublin Calling at Punchestown in May.

On that occasion, the Fame And Glory gelding was ridden with restraint in the rear of mid-division but caught the eye when making good progress to close on the leaders after the fourth from home. Jumping well, he continued to make ground and chased the three-length leader turning into the home straight before accelerating on the run to the last where Noel McParlan spied a stride. Responding with a big leap, Paudie touched down with momentum, allowing him to edge into a narrow advantage only to run out of steam up the run-in and drop back to second spot, eventually crossing the line two lengths adrift of the winner.

That was a promising effort, but he was subsequently purchased for a very modest £25,000 at the Goffs Doncaster Sale in August, and now enters training with Max Young.

From a lovely family and a half-brother to five winners, including Oliver Sherwood's Icing On The Cake (2m chase), Neil Mulholland's Rainy Day Dylan (bumper/2m & 2m 2f hurdle), Karen McLintock's Gurkha Brave (2m-2m 4f hurdle/chase), Graeme McPherson's Calum Gilhooley (bumper/2m 2f & 2m 5f hurdle) and Royal Coburg (bumper).

Given his family all had the speed to win over two miles and he's by Fame And Glory, I would expect Paudie to have the requisite pace to make his presence felt in the 2m hurdle division, or a bumper, should connections choose to go down that route. He may be one for handicaps.

PAY THE PILOT
4YO BAY GELDING

TRAINER:	Kim Bailey
PEDIGREE:	Telescope – Becky B (Alflora)
FORM (P2P NHF):	2 -
OPTIMUM TRIP:	2m 4f +
GOING:	Soft/Heavy

An attractive gelding from the first crop of Telescope.

Pay The Pilot attracted plenty of market support in the lead-up to his racecourse debut in a point-to-point bumper at Punchestown back in March for handler Sean Doyle and was sent off at odds of 100/30 in the hands of Jack Hendrick.

Only a few lengths covered the field for most of the 2m 4f trip with Pay The Pilot happy to sit towards the rear of the group before making a bold move up the inside rail approaching the turn for home. Muscling his way through a gap and showing a bright turn of foot, the four-year-old quickly took up the running, moving into a two- or three-length lead only to be collared with a furlong to race and dropped to third place. Not one to shirk a battle, he stuck to his task gamely and regained the runner-up spot before the line to finish a length and a half behind Last Quarter.

This was a promising debut from Pay The Pilot and had he been held on to a little longer he may have used his turn of foot to better effect on the run-in. Being a half-brother to Bob Buckler's Unwin VC, Pay The Pilot is sure to need a trip to be seen to best effect, probably sooner rather than later. His dam's half-sister, Lord Generous, was also a winner over 3m 1f whilst his other half-sister, Lady Karina, won over 2m 5f and was out of the top hurdler Lady Rebecca.

Pay The Pilot will now be trained by Kim Bailey having been purchased for £130,000 at Cheltenham's March Sale by Aiden Murphy acting on his behalf.

Deep ground will likely bring out the best in him.

PEMBROKE
4YO BAY GELDING

TRAINER:	TBC
PEDIGREE:	Blue Bresil – Moyliscar (Terimon)
FORM:	2 -
OPTIMUM TRIP:	2m +
GOING:	Soft

A major eye-catcher on his only start to date.

Pembroke shaped with more than a degree of promise when coming home with seemingly plenty more in the tank, four lengths adrift of A Fortune Out West, on his debut in a four-year-old geldings' maiden at Punchestown in late May.

Always towards the rear, the gelding was ponderous but safe over his fences, including the fourth from home where he pecked on landing and then at the next where he got in close, causing him to drop to last place. Pushed back into the bridle but not losing any impetus, he continued to catch the eye and made ground easily on the run to the penultimate fence where he was left in fourth place.

Still with over five lengths to find with the eventual winner, he was gently coaxed into the bridle turning for home and despite meeting the last all wrong and landing flat-footed, he picked up in good style to overtake his two nearest pursuers with the minimal amount of fuss and crossed the line in second spot.

This was a very promising display, and he looks certain of finding improvement when required. He's a half-brother to five winners including Miss Night Owl (bumper/2m hurdle), Fighting Fit (2m hurdle), Molly Carew (2m-2m 5f chase) and In By Midnight (2m hurdle). His dam was a maiden chaser but is a half-sister to bumper/2m 4f-3m hurdle winner Sashenka.

Pembroke's family suggests he may have the requisite pace for bumpers or 2m hurdles, but on the little evidence to hand, he shaped as more of a stayer. Softer ground could also suit him as he possesses a round knee action.

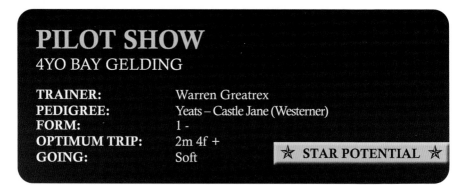

PILOT SHOW
4YO BAY GELDING

TRAINER:	Warren Greatrex
PEDIGREE:	Yeats – Castle Jane (Westerner)
FORM:	1 -
OPTIMUM TRIP:	2m 4f +
GOING:	Soft

★ STAR POTENTIAL ★

This flashy sort should improve plenty for further experience.

Pilot Show made his debut for Tom Weston in the hands of Luke Scott in a three-mile maiden at Garthorpe in April, where ground conditions were probably quicker than ideal when drying out to good to firm from the initial good (watered).

Nevertheless, Pilot Show travelled strongly throughout the race and made headway to chase the leaders on the final circuit before moving up to challenge down the back straight. Jumping into a share of the lead at the third from home, he then quickened on the downhill bend into the straight but made a terrible blunder at the penultimate fence when idling.

Strongly ridden, the gelding recovered well but was awfully green on the run to the last and dived over the fence before somehow managing to stay in front all the way to the line to win by a diminishing three parts of a length from Go On Chez.

That horse has since given no end of boosts to the form – winning three times, including twice under Rules for Oliver Greenall. The fifth, Forty Acres, gave further substance to the form by winning his next start.

Pilot Show is a strongly built model and is a half-brother to Mel Rowley's Castle Keep who showed promise on bumper debut earlier this year. His dam is an unraced half-sister to the very useful 2m 4f-3m hurdle/chase winner King's Odyssey and 2m 7f/3m hurdle winner Sandymount Rose from the family of French 2m 6f Grade 2 winner Lord Carmont.

Everything about Pilot Show screams stamina. He's also likely to flourish when he encounters softer ground. He could be a real dark horse for Warren Greatrex.

PIMLICO POINT
4YO CHESTNUT GELDING

TRAINER:	Kerry Lee
PEDIGREE:	Flemensfirth – Royale Flag (Nickname)
FORM:	1
OPTIMUM TRIP:	2m 4f +
GOING:	Soft

This ex-Colin Bowe-trained gelding looks like a proper horse and now resides at Kerry Lee's base having passed through the ring at Cheltenham's May Sale for a sum of £160,000.

The well-bred son of Flemensfirth created a good impression when stretching clear up the run-in to win by three lengths from Glencorrib Sky on his pointing debut at Ballindenisk in May. Never too far from the pace, the scopey chestnut was asked to knuckle down approaching the second from home and was willing in response, jumping the fence with a slender advantage before asserting on the run to the last. From there the race was in safekeeping and he appeared to cross the line with far more in hand than the winning margin suggests.

Pimlico Point is a big horse for a first foal and comes from a smart family with his dam winning a Grade 1 over fences in France. She is a half-sister to the very useful 2m 3f-3m 2f hurdle/chase winner Mr Mix and 2m 6f Listed Chase winner Mister Bali.

Given his scope, Pimlico Point may take time to come to hand, but the early signs are that he's a promising horse with a bright future. He'll be well suited to galloping tracks.

Pimlico Point – a strong type with plenty of scope (photo by Tattersalls)

PULL AGAIN GREEN
5YO BAY GELDING

TRAINER:	Fergal O'Brien
PEDIGREE:	Kalanisi – Clogher Valley (Oscar)
FORM:	P6F -
FORM (P2P NHF):	1 -
OPTIMUM TRIP:	2m +
GOING:	Good to Soft

Here is another horse that took advantage of a point-to-point bumper during the Covid restrictions.

Pull Again Green weakened quickly and eventually pulled up before the penultimate fence on his pointing debut for handler David O'Brien at Castletown-Geoghegan back in October 2020 but fared much better three weeks later at Dromahane when finishing sixth, shaping like a horse stretched by the trip but was beaten only nine lengths by the Philip Fenton-trained Carrolls Cottage, who has since won twice over hurdles and is now rated 130.

Pull Again Green then went to Mainstown in December where, again, he shaped with a good amount of potential, this time always close to the pace and looking likely to play a strong part in the finish when moving menacingly up to challenge at the second from home, only to land awkwardly and exit the race with a heavy fall.

Having switched yards to Harley Dunne – better known as a jockey – Pull Again Green reappeared in March to compete in a point-to-point bumper over 2m 2f at Wexford, attracting support in the market and going off at odds of 8/1.

Tracking the pace throughout, the Kalanisi gelding raced with ears pricked and was patient to challenge when the pace increased three furlongs from home. Quickening smartly and showing a good attitude inside the two marker, Pull Again Green moved alongside the leader inside the final furlong and had matters in control as he crossed the line with a length and a quarter to spare over the 6/4 favourite Gris Gris Top.

By Kalanisi out of an Oscar mare and a half-brother to Donald McCain's Pull Green, this gelding has enough pace to win another bumper for Fergal O'Brien, but equally he should prove effective in 2m maiden/novice hurdles. He may be best on good, or good to soft ground. He has a lovely enthusiasm in his races.

QUEENS RIVER
5YO BAY MARE

TRAINER:	Nicky Henderson
PEDIGREE:	Kayf Tara – Follow My Leader (Supreme Leader)
FORM:	1 -
OPTIMUM TRIP:	2m 4f +
GOING:	Soft

★ STAR POTENTIAL ★

Queens River hails from a very good family and should be near the top of anyone's horses to follow list as she enters training in the colours of J P McManus.

The strongly built daughter of Kayf Tara was one of seven newcomers in the ten-runner line-up when embarking on her debut in a four-year-old mares' maiden at Boulta in December for handler Aidan Fitzgerald and was reportedly the standout in the paddock.

Given a confident ride from the front by Derek O'Connor, the mare set a sensible pace in the testing conditions and always looked in control of matters despite lacking a little fluency over her fences as the race developed down the far side of the track. Receiving gentle persuasion from the saddle after taking the penultimate fence, the mare quickly came back on the bridle and found an extra gear to regain the lead from Getaway Lily Bear on the short run to the last where she produced one of her best leaps of the race before quickening in smart style on the run to the line to record a very easy three-and-a-half-length success.

The manner with which Queens River travelled and put the race to bed in a matter of strides is indicative of a very smart performer and it was of little surprise to see her sell for a hefty £330,000 at the Goffs UK December sale with the final bid going the way of Kieran McManus.

Queens River is a full sister to the sadly ill-fated smart 2m-2m 3f chase winner The Long Mile and Philip Hobbs' useful 2m 4f hurdle winner Larkbarrow Lad. Her dam unplaced in bumpers but is a half-sister to the 2m-3m 1f hurdle/smart chase winner Master Of The Hall and Pairofbrowneyes.

Queens River has plenty of raw ability and has the potential to develop into a very smart stayer. She appeared to relish the soft ground at Boulta and should be placed to great effect over hurdles by her patient trainer.

RAMBO T
4YO BAY GELDING

TRAINER:	Olly Murphy
PEDIGREE:	Ocovango – Biddy's Boru (Brian Boru)
FORM:	42
OPTIMUM TRIP:	2m 4f +
GOING:	Soft

This son of Ocovango has shown enough promise on both starts between the flags to suggest a victory under Rules won't be far away.

Rambo T shaped with promise when fourth, beaten just over five lengths, by Phantom Getaway at Lisronagh in May, staying on well and closing on the third all the way to the line with just over a length separating him from the second. That looked a good-standard race which clocked a time 11 seconds faster than average and the winner has subsequently joined Kim Bailey to the tune of £90,000.

Three weeks later at Ballingarry, the gelding emerged with even greater credit when finishing a neck second after helping to force the searching gallop before being left in front at the third from home. Doing his utmost to maintain his advantage despite being ridden around the home bend, the gelding displayed a defiant attitude but was outpointed by the cannily ridden Andys Flame who came from well off the pace to win by a neck, stopping the clock 16 seconds quicker than the day's average.

Rambo T has run two tremendous races in defeat and ought to find success in his first season under Rules for Olly Murphy, who picked him up at the Tattersalls May Sale for £50,000.

Being out of a dam by Brian Boru, stamina is going to be of the essence for this gelding.

SCOTCH ON DA ROCKS
4YO BAY GELDING

TRAINER:	Ben Pauling
PEDIGREE:	Fame And Glory – Final Episode (Definite Article)
FORM:	1 -
OPTIMUM TRIP:	2m 4f +
GOING:	Soft

A potentially useful gelding by Fame And Glory.

Scotch On Da Rocks left a lasting impression when coming home the clear-cut winner of the 4&5yo maiden over 2m 4f at Mollington, Oxfordshire, in April for his locally based trainer Tom Ellis. Settled in second place for most of the race, the four-year-old travelled smoothly and produced some excellent leaps before quickening to challenge for the lead on the descent to the second from home.

An untidy leap at that fence knocked him back to second but although clearly green, he knuckled down well on the run to the last, meeting the fence on a good stride and getting away quickly before stretching clear on the run-in, eventually crossing the line with more in hand than the one-and-three-quarter-length winning margin suggests. The third, who was over a further three lengths back, has since come out and won his maiden.

After the race, Tom Ellis said, "He's got size, scope, looks and his sire is on fire. But he's as green as any I've run – we haven't been able to school him as much as I'd like and he's a slow burner, who'll improve a lot for today."

His jockey Jack Andrews went on to say, "He was straightforward and jumped well but was clueless in between his fences and didn't really know how to gallop! But the further he went, the more he got into his stride and he winged the last."

Sold to Highflyer Bloodstock for £80,000 at Cheltenham's April Sale, the gelding has now made his way to Ben Pauling's yard.

Out of an unraced half-sister to the useful winners Treacle (2m-3m 2f hurdle/chase), Green Belt Flyer (2m-3m hurdle/chase) and Lucky Bay (2m 6f hurdle/3m chase).

Scotch On Da Rocks looks like a lovely long-term project. They may give him a spin in a bumper for experience, but I fully expect him to flourish when upped in trip to 2m 4f + over hurdles and later fences.

Scotch On Da Rocks – a lovely long-term project for Ben Pauling (photo by Neale Blackburn)

SEE A STRIDE
4YO BAY FILLY

TRAINER: Gordon Elliott
PEDIGREE: Notnowcato – Steel Glory (Flemensfirth)
FORM: 1 -
OPTIMUM TRIP: 2m 4f +
GOING: Good to Soft

There was plenty to like about the defiant attitude shown by See A Stride when staying on well to win on her pointing debut at Broughshane back in May, not only winning in the quickest time set on the day but stopping the clock 12 seconds faster than the five-year-old geldings' maiden half an hour later.

See A Stride was only one of two fillies to make up the ten-runner field but she travelled strongly throughout the contest and showed the geldings a clean pair of heels to pull clear from the back of the last under a power-packed drive from Michael Sweeney to win by one and a half lengths from Hold Onto The Line who was benefiting from experience.

By Notnowcato out of an unraced sister to Colin Tizzard's bumper and 2m hurdle winner Old Tricks and also Nicky Richards' useful 2m 4f-3m 1f hurdle/chase winner (and Listed-placed chaser) According To John.

Now in the care of Gordon Elliott having been purchased by Aiden Murphy standing alongside the trainer at Cheltenham's May Sale for £47,000. This filly has already shown ability and ought to do well when the emphasis is on stamina.

SERIOUS CHARGES
4YO BAY GELDING

TRAINER:	Anthony Honeyball
PEDIGREE:	Soldier Of Fortune – South West Nine (Oscar)
FORM:	2 -
OPTIMUM TRIP:	2m 4f +
GOING:	Good/Soft

Serious Charges showed plenty of ability on his sole start to date when chasing home Cool Survivor at Cork in April and there looks to be more to come from this promising individual.

The Soldier Of Fortune gelding travelled well throughout the race under Jamie Scallan but just lacked a little bit of natural pace when the leading pair upped the tempo on the run to the third from home. Sticking to his task in taking fashion, the four-year-old was able to latch back on to the duo on the charge to the penultimate fence and moved into second spot when the weakening Ballycamus departed the race.

Continuing to respond to pressure, he tried his best to close on the leader, Cool Survivor, but couldn't find the extra gear necessary to get on terms and was eventually beaten a comfortable four lengths.

Quite an imposing sort of horse and far more stoutly bred than his conqueror, Serious Charges looks the sort who will benefit from plenty of time. He's closely related to Outrageous Romana, a 2m4f-2m7f hurdle winner. He is also a half-brother to the 2m2f hurdle winner Cosa Ban and 2m1f-2m4f hurdle winner Urban Dusk. His dam was a winner over 2m on both the Flat and over hurdles.

Purchased by Anthony Honeyball at Cheltenham's April Sale for £85,000, he will likely start in a bumper, but I fully expect we won't see the best of him until tried over further once hurdling.

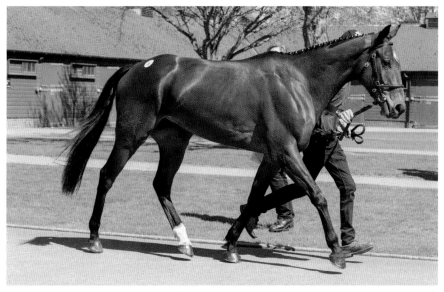

Serious Charges – has plenty more to offer now in the care of Anthony Honeyball (photo by Tattersalls)

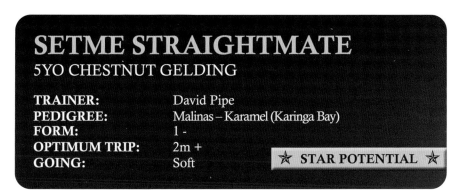

SETME STRAIGHTMATE
5YO CHESTNUT GELDING

TRAINER:	David Pipe
PEDIGREE:	Malinas – Karamel (Karinga Bay)
FORM:	1 -
OPTIMUM TRIP:	2m +
GOING:	Soft

☆ **STAR POTENTIAL** ☆

A very impressive winner of his only start to date.

Setme Straightmate couldn't have made it look any easier when coasting home the 12-length winner of a point-to-point at Boulta back in December for Mary Doyle in the colours of Baltimore Stables.

The ground, which was officially described as soft/heavy, looked awfully churned up but that didn't stop this gelding from travelling well within his comfort zone before easily upping the ante after a slick jump over the third from home, taking half a dozen lengths out of the field. Still hard on the bridle and going further clear by the time he rose over the penultimate fence, he had more than enough up his sleeve on the short run to the last, which he jumped a little leg-weary, before pulling away again on the run to the line.

Not only did this look visually impressive, but the clock recorded a time 14 seconds quicker than the day's average – ten seconds or more faster than any other race.

A half-brother to the 2m 4f hurdle winner Queen Jesse Jay, his dam is an unraced half-sister to bumper/fairly useful 2m 3f-2m 3f hurdle winner Carlton Jack and point winner/2m and 2m5f hurdle winner U B Carefull.

David Pipe has enjoyed tremendous success with graduates from this operation and the impression which Setme Straightmate created suggests the Pond House trainer has another top prospect on his hands.

SHOLOKJACK
5YO BAY GELDING

TRAINER:	Paul Nicholls
PEDIGREE:	Sholokhov – Another Pet (Un Desperado)
FORM:	1 -
OPTIMUM TRIP:	2m +
GOING:	Good to Soft

A strong traveller with a useful turn of foot.

Sholokjack highlighted himself as a decent prospect when coming clear in the hands of Derek O'Connor to win the opening division of the four-year-olds' maiden at Mainstown in December for Ellmarie Holden, recording the fastest time set on the day – seven seconds quicker than standard and four seconds faster than the second division.

Always travelling stylishly, the son of Sholokhov made ground easily to chase the leaders down the far side of the track and although not the most fluent over his fences, his momentum remained uninterrupted as he loomed up to challenge turning for home. Left in the lead at the penultimate fence when Aucunrisque fell, he then asserted his advantage on the run to the last, opening up a healthy advantage on his nearest pursuer and jumping the fences well before powering to the line to record a comfortable two-length success over Creative Control.

The form has taken a few knocks since, but the horse which fell two from home showed up well to finish second on his debut for Chris Gordon in a Stratford bumper. I'd also be confident of Sholokjack finding improvement when he brushes up his jumping.

By Sholokhov out of an Un Desperado mare, he's a half-brother to the useful 2m 6f-3m chase winner Another Stowaway and 2m 2f hurdle winner Aurora's Dream. His dam failed to show a great deal in her races but is a half-sister to the smart 2m-3m chase winner Super Tactics.

Not short of pace, Paul Nicholls could start him in a bumper, but he has the size to develop into a decent staying chaser in time.

SINGASONGSAM
4YO BAY GELDING

TRAINER:	Dr Richard Newland
PEDIGREE:	Black Sam Bellamy – Vin Rose (Alflora)
FORM:	3 - 1
OPTIMUM TRIP:	2m +
GOING:	Good

An impressive last-time-out winner.

Singasongsam shaped with promise when filling third spot, beaten only three lengths, by two more experienced rivals on his pointing debut over 3m at Garthorpe back in April, making a challenge at the second from home but hanging badly to his left and lacking the extra gear needed to get on terms in the closing stages.

Dropped back in trip to 2m 4f for division two of the maiden at Hexham three weeks later, the gelding was given a good ride by John Dawson who held him up in the early stages before making good progress on the final circuit.

Travelling powerfully, the son of Black Sam Bellamy was undeterred by a slow leap over the third from home and readily recovered the lost ground, latching back on to the heels of the leaders before displaying a dazzling turn of foot to scoot to the lead on the home bend.

From there the race was in no doubt as he pinged the penultimate fence and extended his advantage with the minimal amount of fuss on the run to the last before one final measured leap allowed him to cruise clear up the run-in to record a very easy 12-length success over Universal Run with a further ten lengths back to the third.

Sent to the Goffs UK Spring Sale at Doncaster in May, he was purchased by Dr Richard Newland for what looks to be a bargain at £35,000.

A half-brother to the 2m 7f-3m 2f chase winner The Late Legend. His dam placed over 2m and is a half-sister to the bumper/2m 7f-3m 3f hurdle winner Wyfield Rose from the further family of the smart staying hurdler Rose Ravine.

This is a horse with plenty of pace and a naturally high cruising speed. He will likely start off in bumpers this term but expect improvement when he enters races where the emphasis is on stamina. Good ground suits him.

SPORTING ACE
5YO BAY GELDING

TRAINER:	Neil King
PEDIGREE:	Shantou – Knockbounce View (Old Vic)
FORM:	2 -
OPTIMUM TRIP:	2m +
GOING:	Soft

Sporting Ace looks a great addition to Neil King's stable.

The Shantou gelding made his debut for Matthew Flynn O'Connor in a four-year-old maiden at Lingstown in November where he came home in second spot behind the subsequent £430,000 Cheveley Park purchase Grangeclare West, who has already franked the form by coming home the nine-length winner on bumper debut at Punchestown for Willie Mullins.

The maiden was a rough race with a whole host of challengers in with a chance at the fourth from home, but despite Sporting Ace missing out in the jumping stakes and losing his pitch, he was soon back on an even keel, showing a good attitude and plenty of speed before jumping into a challenging position over the next. From there, he made a sweeping move around horses, taking him into second position before jumping the penultimate fence a length adrift of Grangeclare West with King Kal also in there challenging.

The trio really began to motor from that point with Sporting Ace doing his best to get on terms, but despite mastering the battle with the eventual third, he couldn't find the extra gear needed to go with Grangeclare West who eased clear after the last to win by four lengths.

Purchased by Stroud Coleman Bloodstock on behalf of Neil King, he certainly looks a value buy at £90,000 when you consider how much the winner went for. He also boasts a strong pedigree being a full brother to dual bumper winner Eilise's A Lady. His dam is an unraced sister to the top-class chaser Our Vic.

Sporting Ace looks like an above-average horse and may start in a bumper before progressing to hurdles. He was entered at Warwick in the spring, but connections must have decided to give him more time.

SUPER SURVIVOR
5YO BAY GELDING

TRAINER:	Jamie Snowden
PEDIGREE:	Shantou – All The Best Mate (Alflora)
FORM:	2
OPTIMUM TRIP:	2m 4f +
GOING:	Soft

Super Survivor's debut at Dromahane in May was always going to be one to watch after fetching €70,000 as a three-year-old at the Tattersalls Derby Sale in June 2019, selling to Monbeg Stables.

Donnchadh Doyle's five-year-old moved comfortably just off the pace but made a bad mistake at the sixth last, costing him both ground and momentum. Recovering well and ridden wide around the turn into the straight, he loomed up to challenge for a three-way share of the lead at the third from home and upped the tempo on the charge to the next. Unable to shake off the attention of the long-time leader, barely a whisker separated the pair as they took the final two fences, but it was the more experienced Tigers Roar who managed to bob his head at the right time on the line.

Super Survivor's mistake happened far enough from home that it probably didn't have a bearing on the result, but he certainly showed enough here to suggest victory won't be far away.

Sold at the Goffs UK Spring Sale to Tom Malone standing alongside Jamie Snowden for £115,000, he is a half-brother to the point winner Bitofalright. His dam is a hurdle winner and a half-sister to the 3m 1f chase winner The Tin Miner with the further family linking back to the triple Gold Cup winner Best Mate.

There's a lot to like about Super Survivor. He'll probably be seen in the best light when the emphasis is on stamina. Soft ground is also likely to suit.

TANGO TARA
5YO BAY GELDING

TRAINER:	Paul Nicholls
PEDIGREE:	Kayf Tara – Bling Noir (Moscow Society)
FORM:	1 -
OPTIMUM TRIP:	2m 4f +
GOING:	Soft/Heavy

★ **STAR POTENTIAL** ★

Tango Tara looks like another top recruit to graduate from Baltimore Stables.

Mary Doyle's son of Kayf Tara proved stamina was no issue when staying on resolutely over the final couple of fences to get the better of the well-regarded Upping The Anti – subsequently finished sixth in a bumper for Henry de Bromhead – on his debut in a four-year-olds' maiden at Ballindenisk last November.

Always up with the pace, the gelding travelled smoothly in the hands of John O'Neill before overtaking the long-time leader and eventual second on the run to the penultimate fence. Forced to battle, he knuckled down in good style and despite diving over the last he had plenty left in the reserves to pull two lengths clear on the run to the line, in turn clocking a time 14 seconds quicker than standard – two seconds faster than the second division won by the subsequent ultra-impressive bumper winner, Journey With Me.

Tango Tara is a physically imposing individual, typical of the type Paul Nicholls does very well with, and it was him who stood alongside Tom Malone who shelled out £120,000 at the Goffs Sale in December to take him home.

A half-brother to Henry Daly's strong stayer Rapper (2m 5f and 2m 7f hurdle winner) out of a once-raced French sister to Louis Loire (2m 2f and 2m 4f chase winner). His further family links back to the Topham runner-up Katnap.

I would imagine Tango Tara will take time to reach full physical development and consequently we won't see the best of him for another season or more. That said, success in the staying hurdle division can be expected before he goes novice chasing.

THE KING OF RYHOPE
5YO CHESTNUT GELDING

TRAINER:	Dan Skelton
PEDIGREE:	Malinas – Eleven Fifty Nine (Midnight Legend)
FORM:	1 -
OPTIMUM TRIP:	2m +
GOING:	Soft

This gelding demonstrated a straightforward attitude when getting the better of a fiercely contested 16-runner four-year-olds' maiden at Lingstown last November – a race where the time compared favourably with the others on the card, including division one of the opening maiden which saw Grangeclare West – subsequently purchased for £430,000 – clock a time two seconds slower than this gelding.

After making the early running, The King Of Ryhope settled on to the heels of the leaders where he jumped well and travelled within his comfort zone. With a circuit to travel, the entire field was still standing and tightly grouped but the eye was drawn to this son of Malinas as he produced exuberant leaps, including at the fourth from home where he came up out of Declan Lavery's hands.

From there, he angled for a better position and moved closer to the pace as the field fragmented before another splendid leap over the penultimate fence allowed him to land alongside the leader. Encouraged to poke his nose to the front and finding an extra gear on the descent, he'd opened up a healthy advantage by the time he'd reached the last, which was fortunate as he took a good look at it before making a terrible blunder. Recovering well, he picked up again to cross the line with one and a half lengths to spare over Supreme Yeats.

That looks good form, with the runner-up showing ability under Rules for Laura Morgan, whilst the third and fourth went on to place again in points.

Purchased for £75,000 by Ryan Mahon, The King Of Ryhope is the second foal out of Anthony Honeyball's Listed bumper and 2m hurdle winner Eleven Fifty Nine.

On the little evidence to hand, there's enough to suggest this gelding can follow in his dam's footsteps and win a bumper, although given how well he jumped bar the mishap at the last, connections may be keen to press on over hurdles.

THE QUESTIONER
5YO CHESTNUT GELDING

TRAINER:	Oliver Greenall
PEDIGREE:	Ask – Cush Bach (Bach)
FORM:	2 -
OPTIMUM TRIP:	2m 4f +
GOING:	Soft

This horse is a slow burner but has the physical scope to develop into a useful staying chaser.

The son of Ask made his debut at Tipperary in April and caught the eye by finishing with a real late rattle to grab second place, six lengths behind Coachman who has since fetched £140,000 at the Cheltenham April Sale when selling the way of Marcus Collie and Oliver Signy.

Everything appeared to be happening too quickly for The Questioner as he was nudged into the bridle at various stages of the race before being ridden more vigorously approaching the third from home which he jumped last but one of the eight that remained. From there he continued to be cajoled but gradually passed rivals and really picked up the bit after the last to overtake the eventual third who went on to boost the form by winning his next start by six lengths. The Boola Boss, who was beaten over 45 lengths into sixth place, also helped give the form some substance by finishing second, beaten three lengths, on his next start.

The Questioner is a good-looking gelding but is very much a horse in need of time to fully develop. When on parade at the Doncaster Spring Sale, the strength in his front quarters didn't translate to his hindquarters. That will come and Oliver Greenall, who parted with £40,000, could find that's money well spent.

The chestnut also boasts a strong pedigree being out of an unraced half-sister to Noel Meade's Grade 2-winning hurdler and Grade 1-placed chaser Monksland, who also won two bumpers. Other family members include five-time winner Bobcatbilly and Neil Mulholland's Lord Accord.

Soft ground and a trip in excess of 2m 4f ought to be the making of this strong stayer.

The Questioner – could look an excellent purchase for £40,000 (photo by JTW Equine Photography)

THE REAL JET
5YO CHESTNUT MARE

TRAINER:	Andy Irvine
PEDIGREE:	Jet Away – Stonehouse (Snurge)
FORM:	31 -
OPTIMUM TRIP:	2m +
GOING:	Good to Soft

The Real Jet is a lovely project for her lower-profile base.

This flashy white-faced daughter of Jet Away shaped with plenty of encouragement when staying on well into third spot on her debut at Borris House last November, jumping well and latching on to the leaders at the fourth from home before finishing one-paced in the closing stages.

Putting that experience to good use when next seen the following month at Moig South, The Real Jet was always on the pace and pressed on with over a circuit to travel before being joined for the lead after the fourth from home. Faced with a sustained duel as She's So Lovely raced with her over the next couple of fences, this five-year-old showed a truly admirable attitude in the closing stages, digging deep into her stamina reserves up the short run-in to eventually cross the line with two and a half lengths in hand.

The Real Jet may not turn out to be a world-beater, but she's very game and looks well bought by Andy Irvine for £35,000.

A half-sister to Nicky Henderson's bumper winner, Welsby. Her dam is a 2m 3f chase/2m 4f hurdle winner out of a half-sister to bumper/2m 4f-3m hurdle/ useful chase winner Princess Symphony.

Given the natural pace she demonstrated in her races, teamed with her pedigree, The Real Jet may be capable of winning a bumper before embarking on a career over hurdles. Watch out for her at somewhere like Plumpton or Fakenham.

TIME FOR BELL
5YO BAY MARE

TRAINER:	Christian Williams
PEDIGREE:	Mahler – Bell Walks Eve (Flemensfirth)
FORM:	2
OPTIMUM TRIP:	2m 4f +
GOING:	Soft

★ **STAR POTENTIAL** ★

This daughter of Mahler created a good impression when chasing home Colin Bowe's newcomer, Dooyork, at Tattersalls Farm in May; a race that looked above average and saw 14 runners go to post.

Time For Bell caught the eye throughout and leapt into second spot at the fourth from home before being ridden along after the next where she jumped untidily. Responding to her jockey's urgings, she knuckled down well and cleared the penultimate fence in good style before bridging the gap with the front-runner on the turn into the straight.

Sandwiched between the long-time leader and the eventual winner, who came with a sweeping run from off the pace, Time For Bell was bumped for a stride or two and forced to switch wide before jumping the last in third spot. Continuing to demonstrate her willingness, she battled bravely on the run-in and regained second spot before crossing the line one and a half lengths adrift of the winner, with a head to spare over the third.

That was a fine effort considering the mistake at a crucial stage in the race together with the interference she suffered before the last. The form has also worked out well with the third winning on her next start, whilst the fifth, who was beaten ten lengths, came out and won by 15 lengths on their next start.

Time For Bell looks an honest galloper, and she's also very well bred being out of an unraced sister to the bumper/high-class hurdle/chase winner (2m 3f-3m 1f) Time For Rupert and the very useful bumper/2m 6f hurdle/chase winner Minella Fair.

She's ultimately a staying chaser for the seasons to come, but in the interim she looks an exciting prospect to follow over hurdles.

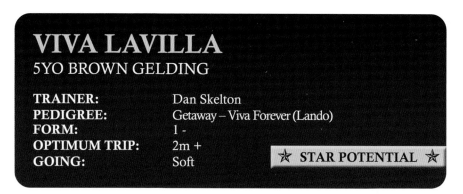

VIVA LAVILLA
5YO BROWN GELDING

TRAINER:	Dan Skelton
PEDIGREE:	Getaway – Viva Forever (Lando)
FORM:	1 -
OPTIMUM TRIP:	2m +
GOING:	Soft

☆ **STAR POTENTIAL** ☆

This fine, big raw chaser made a stylish winning debut in the hands of Jamie Codd for trainer Denis Murphy in a highly competitive four-year-old geldings' maiden at Lingstown – a victory which clocked a time five seconds quicker than the first division which was won by the subsequent £430,000 Cheveley Park purchase, Grangeclare West.

The eye was constantly drawn to Viva Lavilla as he tracked the leaders throughout before producing a breathtaking leap over the fourth from home. From there he slowly edged closer to the pace before laying down a stronger challenge over the penultimate fence.

Cruising into second place despite looking unbalanced down the hill, he then quickened impressively once he hit the level ground and moved upsides the leader on the approach to the final fence, where one final tremendous leap allowed him to touch down with an advantage before finally getting the upper hand on the gallant second in the closing stages to win by a length.

This really was a performance that made you sit up and take note, not only because of the fast time, but because the form has worked out well. The third, who was beaten 16 lengths, was beaten under a length at Lisronagh in May and Bravo Team, who was pulled up after the third from home, came out and won his next start by an easy eight lengths.

The son of Getaway doesn't boast the strongest of pedigrees, although his full brother showed ability when finishing second in a bumper on his only start to date for Jamie Snowden. His dam was a French 10.5f and 1m 3f Flat winner before winning a low-key hurdle race over 2m 1f for Alex Hales.

Given Viva Lavilla's tall stature, it's all credit to his natural ability that not only was he able to show so much on debut, but to win in the manner which he did. He hasn't been seen since but has probably taken time to come to hand.

Blessed with both speed and stamina, he can have a fruitful career over hurdles before developing into a smart staying chaser. Galloping tracks where he can use his long stride will see him in the best light.

WATCH HOUSE CROSS
4YO BAY GELDING

TRAINER:	TBC
PEDIGREE:	Libertarian – Benefit Lodge (Beneficial)
FORM:	1 -
OPTIMUM TRIP:	2m +
GOING:	Soft

Watch House Cross showed plenty of promise when chasing home the potentially very useful Harry Des Ongrais on his debut at Fairyhouse in April, making most of the running and matching strides with the winner all the way to the home straight before being left behind before the last, eventually crossing the line ten lengths down in second but ten lengths clear of the third.

Benefiting from both the experience and race fitness, Watch House Cross went to Dromahane two weeks later and returned the easy five-length winner from the newcomer Garcon Dargent, making all the running and producing a confident round of jumping before staying on strongly to the line.

Possibly better suited to going right-handed, having jumped out to his left on debut, this was a professional performance from the four-year-old and the form has since been franked by the third who won next time by an easy seven lengths, whilst Rodaniche, who fell when in contention three from home, finished a good second on his next start.

From the family of top-class jumper Dorans Pride, Watch House Cross doesn't lack pace but possesses a sizable frame and ought to develop into a nice chaser in time.

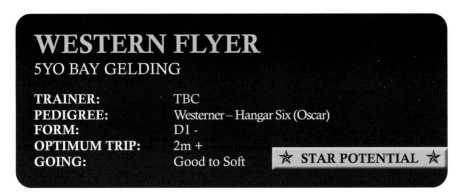

WESTERN FLYER
5YO BAY GELDING

TRAINER:	TBC
PEDIGREE:	Westerner – Hangar Six (Oscar)
FORM:	D1 -
OPTIMUM TRIP:	2m +
GOING:	Good to Soft

★ STAR POTENTIAL ★

Western Flyer was disqualified due to Eoin Mahon failing to weigh in after finishing a promising third behind subsequent Punchestown bumper winner, My Mate Mozzie, on his debut at Tattersalls Farm in December.

Back with a bang at Tipperary in April in the hands of Derek O'Connor, Western Flyer produced a thoroughly professional performance, travelling powerfully behind the leaders before quickening into the wings of the third from home and touching down with a one-length lead. Striding out with purpose, the bay could have been called the winner a long way from home as he extended further clear on the long run to the penultimate fence before one final efficient leap over the last sealed the deal and allowed him to cruise up the run-in with ears pricked to cross the line by three very easy lengths from Gredin, with four lengths back to Whelans Bridge.

The winning distance really doesn't do justice to how easily Western Flyer won. Not only did he cross the line without barely breaking sweat, but he also recorded a time three seconds quicker than standard and the third came out and franked the form by winning next time.

Western Flyer is out of an unraced half-sister to the useful 2m hurdle (including Grade 3) winner Ballynacree, from the further family of smart jumper Risk Accessor.

Unsold for £150,000 at the Goffs Punchestown Sale in April, Western Flyer is currently in the care of Mrs Grainne M O'Connor, but given his potential, I would imagine he'll make his way to one of the top stables before embarking on a career under Rules.

He has both speed and stamina. He's also confident through the air which will stand him in good stead in hurdle races this term.

WHACKER CLAN
5YO BAY GELDING

TRAINER:	TBC
PEDIGREE:	Westerner – Kolaliya (Kahyasi)
FORM:	33 -1
OPTIMUM TRIP:	2m +
GOING:	Good

This progressive gelding could slip under the radar.

Whacker Clan shaped with promise on his debut at Damma House last November when staying on steadily from the rear of the field, despite jumping sketchily, to chase home the now 131-rated Up For Parol with the subsequent 10-length point winner, Git Maker, splitting the two.

He then went to Turtulla a fortnight later and again filled third spot after plugging on all the way to the line despite being off the bridle a long way from home. Ahead of him that day were Grand Jury, a subsequent useful bumper winner for Henry de Bromhead, and Minella Cocooner who made a successful Rules debut for Willie Mullins by winning a bumper by ten lengths.

After a long winter break, Whacker Clan reappeared at Grennan at the end of May in the first division of the five-year-old geldings' maiden where he returned the easy eight-length winner after jumping to the front at the second from home and demonstrating a potent turn of foot towards the last. After a spring-heeled leap there, the race was in no doubt as he scooted up the run-in for a deserved success.

Clearly relishing the good to yielding ground in comparison to the softer underfoot conditions he experienced in the winter, Whacker Clan is certainly a name to watch out for in the early part of the season, or next spring.

From a useful Flat family, his dam is a half-sister to a 1m 2f/2m-2m 4f hurdle winner Kozmina Bay and 1m 6f-2m winner Mina's Boy. His further family links back to the high-class 1m-1m 4f winner Kozana.

Whacker Clan is clearly not devoid of speed and would be interesting in a bumper. He may be one for handicaps further down the line.

Spying the gap (photo by Susie Cahill)

The
POINT-TO-POINT
Recruits 2020/21

THE LOOK BACK

In this feature, I take a look back at last year's recruits, some of which have already showed tremendous promise while others are taking a little longer to come to hand.

That's the beauty of *The Point-To-Point Recruits*, as many of these individuals have the pedigrees and physiques to develop over time and it's exciting to follow their journey, right from the moment they make their debuts under Rules to the time they start to fulfil their potential, at whatever level that may be.

For the third year in a row, I was delighted to have featured the Cheltenham Festival Champion Bumper winner as having 'Star Potential' with this year's renewal going the way of **Sir Gerhard**. Carrying the famous Cheveley Park Stud colours and receiving a masterful ride from Rachael Blackmore, the five-year-old followed in the footsteps of the fellow-owned Ferny Hollow and Envoi Allen.

Sir Gerhard started the season with Gordon Elliott, for whom he won twice, including a clear-cut victory of the Listed Future Champions bumper at Navan before switching to Willie Mullins following the unsavoury circumstances that led to Gordon's disqualification. That switch came on 2 March – a fortnight before the start of the Festival – but it didn't unsettle Sir Gerhard as he came home the half-length winner from his now stable companion Kilcruit, making all and quickening off the home turn and keeping enough in reserve to hold on up the hill.

He possibly didn't run to the same level when beaten in a rematch with Kilcruit at Punchestown's Grade 1 bumper the following month and I imagine he'll stick to the two-mile hurdling division this season, the obvious long-term aim being the Supreme Novices' Hurdle.

Robcour has immense strength in depth with the horses under their banner and **Gerri Colombe** looks ready to step into the limelight over hurdles this season.

The imposing son of Saddler Maker was two from two in bumpers for Gordon Elliott last term, winning by 24 lengths at Fairyhouse and then making all and demonstrating a turn of foot to win under a penalty by just shy of four lengths in what looked on paper to be a good race at Naas in February.

A really classy sort of horse with both speed and stamina, I envisage he'll be best suited to a step up in trip to 2m 4f, and although untried on better ground, he has the action to suggest it won't be a problem. He has the potential to be a Ballymore Novices' Hurdle horse.

Another in Gordon Elliott's yard to win both his bumpers last term was **Hollow Games**.

Owned by Noel and Valerie Moran, the Beat Hollow gelding looked a real stayer en route to success at both Punchestown in November and then Leopardstown's Christmas meeting in December, needing persuasion from the saddle to put the race to bed but on both occasions hitting the line strongly to win with far more in hand then the winning margins suggest.

He'll likely start off over 2m 4f but I wouldn't be surprised if he's tackling three miles by the end of the season. He appears to have a really gritty attitude and may have the ability for something like the Albert Bartlett, depending on how the early part of the season goes.

Another of Robcour's to stay with this season is **Petibonome**.

I had high hopes for the Al Namix gelding last term but despite hitting the paintwork on all three starts, there were plenty of positives to be gleaned and another summer on his back could be just the ticket.

His two-length defeat by Cape Gentleman in a 2m 4f maiden hurdle at Punchestown in December now reads well, with that winner rated on a mark of 140, and he arguably should have won the 2m 3f novice hurdle at Naas when outpointed by the 136-rated You Raised Me Up. He looks an out-and-out stayer and there should be a winning opportunity to be found in the early part of the season, especially if contesting a novice handicap hurdle from a mark of 126.

He will stay three miles and there's still plenty of time for him to reach a decent level, although he'll improve again when sent chasing next season.

Holymacapony, also trained by Henry de Bromhead, looked an exciting prospect when bursting on to the hurdling scene with an eight-length defeat of Gaillard Du Mesnil at Punchestown last November. He lost his way thereafter and pulled up in a Grade 2 over 2m 4f at Navan in December before running down the field in the Grade 1 won by Gaillard Du Mesnil over 2m 6f at Leopardstown in February.

A recent spin to finish third behind Macgiloney in a handicap hurdle over an extended 2m 5f at Galway from a mark of 130 showed some hope of a return to form. He should come on a bundle for that and it's interesting that connections have him out so soon – maybe getting him cherry-ripe for an early-season pot.

Clondaw Bertie is another who's been out early for Henry de Bromhead. He's been disappointing since winning his point-to-point by 12 lengths but he's a big, raw horse and we may not see the best of him until he goes novice chasing next term. In the meantime, he can progress through the handicap ranks, starting on a mark of 109.

I expect **Magic Tricks** to be primed to win a valuable handicap hurdle.

Being a brother to Abacadabras, expectations have been high for this son of Davidoff but since his impressive hurdling debut at Navan last December, you'd have to say he's been disappointing. Like his brother, he doesn't appear the most straightforward, but he went very close to landing a valuable prize at Fairyhouse from a mark of 132 in April, only to be collared by the fellow-owned J P McManus winner, Hearts Are Trumps.

He's now on a mark of 136, and although he finished well down the field in the Galway Hurdle when tried in first-time cheekpieces, he travelled well for a long way and was asked to make ground on a disadvantageous part of the track. He will crop up somewhere, but bookmakers have been on to him the last few times.

Gordon Elliott and J P McManus surely won't be wasting too much time over hurdles with their exciting novice chase prospect **Gars De Sceaux**.

The imposing grey son of Saddler Maker more than likely found the 2m trip a shade too sharp when beaten 12 lengths by Hook Up on his hurdling debut at Fairyhouse last November and appreciated the step up to 2m 4f when battling bravely to shed his maiden tag at Navan in January.

Upped in trip again, this time to 2m 7f on a revisit to Navan in March, he proved far too good for the opposition and returned home the very easy nine-length winner, sluicing through the mud and coming clear after the third from home to win in a canter.

From the family of Bristol De Mai, Gars De Sceaux is every inch a staying chaser. He'll likely start off in an ordinary novice chase, but I expect him to compete at the festivals throughout the season. Maybe he'll end up in the Brown Advisory Novices' Chase or the National Hunt Chase come March.

The Alan Halsall-owned **Minella Escape** also has the potential to develop into a smart novice chaser.

This gelding hit the deck on two of his four starts over hurdles last term, including last time in a Grade 3 over 3m at Navan, but the easy seven-length victory the time before that at Tramore on New Year's Day gave us a glimpse of the natural ability the six-year-old possesses.

With such an imposing physique, hurdles appear to get in the gelding's way, and he'll likely give greater respect to a fence which, together with his obvious ability, bodes well for a fruitful novice chase campaign. He's an exciting individual and he stays well.

Flame Bearer finished second, with his jumping letting him down, on his sole point-to-point for Donnchadh Doyle but made an instant impression in a bumper at Thurles in December when coming clear inside the final couple of furlongs to record a comfortable five-length success for trainer Pat Doyle when sporting a first-time tongue-tie. Proving that was no fluke, he followed up under a penalty at Limerick in March, again cruising through the race before pulling clear up the home straight.

What's so impressive about this gelding is how strongly he powers through a race. He's obviously got a huge engine and can easily develop into an above average hurdler over two miles. Testing ground suits him well, although connections have said he will go on anything.

Brandy Love is another with plenty of speed for the two-mile hurdling division. She was an impressive debut winner in a bumper at Fairyhouse back in December, with her rider very complimentary of her in the post-race interview. She could only manage third behind her stable companion, Grangee, when well fancied next time in a Grade 2 bumper at the Dublin Racing Festival, but that turned out to be very useful form.

Brandy Love was electric over her fences when winning a point-to-point and if she can translate that to hurdles, she has the potential to reach the top of the ladder this season.

Paul Nolan's **Western Zara** is another who can rise up the mares' division. She was the beneficiary when Humble Glory fell at the final flight at Clonmel back in April, but she was plugging on nicely and still in with a chance when the leader departed. Her pedigree suggests she'll be best around two miles but, given the way she travels, I believe she'll stay at least 2m 4f.

Indigo Breeze made an impressive winning Rules debut for Gordon Elliott in a bumper at Thurles last October and finished a short-head second to the fairly useful Keskonrisk in a maiden hurdle at Fairyhouse the following month before being no match for Gaillard Du Mesnil when beaten 72 lengths over 2m 4f at Leopardstown in December. He still has great potential if he can brush up his jumping and is still a novice over hurdles.

Deploy The Getaway was the name on plenty of people's lips after winning his point by 20 lengths back in February 2019. However, a setback kept him off the track for over two years and he was understandably rusty when finishing second on bumper debut at Thurles in March. He can build on that and being only six years old, he remains a horse with a bright future, providing his troubles are behind him. He'll now be sent hurdling.

Corran Cross took time to find the winning formula under Rules and appears to be more at home on the spring/summer ground having won in June and August, the latter occasion over fences at Downpatrick. A mark of 124 may underestimate his ability, especially when he has conditions to suit.

I was excited about the future for **Clondaw Secret**, especially after he made a winning start over hurdles for Gordon Elliott in December. A promising third behind Diol Ker followed, but he has since lost his way and no improvement was found with a switch to fences at Galway in July. He now has something to prove.

Finally on the Irish scene, we were rewarded for our patience with **Street Value** when he landed two hefty gambles, firstly at Clonmel over 2m 3f from a mark of 98 and then secondly at Gowran Park when upped in trip to an extended 2m 4f from 11lb higher. No match for No Grey Area's from a mark of 120 when attempting the hat-trick on a revisit to Gowran in March, he rounded off the season on a mark of 122, but I still believe there's more to come.

Bred to stay forever and completely unexposed over three miles, we could be in for some more fun this winter. Being a six-year-old turning seven, connections may be keen to send him novice handicap chasing.

On to home soil and it was hard not to be impressed with Richard Phillips' **Lesser**, who extended his unbeaten record to four with a very smooth 15-length beating of Lanty Slea over 2m 5f at Kelso in May. That success followed a 25-length victory at Wetherby in March over an extended 2m 3f on hurdle debut having won a bumper over an extended 2m by 11 lengths on heavy ground at Bangor back in December.

Already a seven-year-old, the plan must be to go chasing this season and given his imposing stature, you'd have to be confident that this strong traveller can find further improvement in that sphere. An opening mark of 130 doesn't appear harsh and he's versatile with regards to the ground.

Another in Phillips' yard to stick with is **Robin Des Smoke**.

I'm a big fan of this daughter of Robin Des Pres and she ran two cracking races in defeat at both Wetherby and Plumpton when chasing home Hunny Moon and Wheesht respectively. Given her copious amounts of experience in point-to-points, she could well go straight into a novice handicap chase this term, or she may try a handicap hurdle before switching. A mark of 104 looks well within range and her tenacious attitude is an asset.

Evan Williams enjoyed tremendous success last season and **Star Gate** looks to be a useful younger horse to look forward to.

The Imperial Monarch gelding won his point-to-point for Colin Bowe and announced himself on to the Rules scene with an impressive victory in a maiden hurdle over an extended 2m 3f at Chepstow, beating Everglow by six-and-a-half widening lengths. Fast and fluent over his hurdles, he breezed to the lead after the penultimate flight before staying on strongly to win easily.

Stepped up to Grade 2 company for the Ballymore Winter Novices' Hurdle at Sandown in December, he was a well-backed favourite for the three-runner contest and again impressed with his clean jumping before producing a notable change of gear after the last to come home the impressive eight-and-a-half-length winner from Valleres.

He was then put away for the season after being no match for Bravemansgame when beaten ten lengths in the Grade 1 Challow Novices' Hurdle at Newbury. He will most likely be sent novice chasing this term and can continue to develop into a smart middle-distance performer. He jumped his fences well in his point and copes well with deep mid-winter ground.

Stable companion **Only The Bold** won in dominant style in a novices' hurdle over an extended 2m 4f at Southwell in February but was disappointing back over that course and distance the following month when trailing home 35 lengths behind Cadzand. He's better than that and a mark of 126 could underestimate him. He beat the now 139-rated Tommy's Oscar by nine lengths in a point-to-point and fences could unlock further success.

Donald McCain also has a lovely team of young horses and right up there is **Bareback Jack**.

The Tim Leslie-owned five-year-old showed plenty of natural ability to make a winning Rules debut in a novices' hurdle over an extended 1m 7f at Musselburgh in November on ground which was probably faster than ideal. He then followed that with an impressive fleet-of-foot hurdling display at Catterick in January when beating Tonyx by an easy nine lengths on soft ground over the same trip.

Back to Musselburgh for a Supreme Novices' Hurdle Trial, he lowered the colours of Tommy's Oscar to the tune of two and a quarter lengths, quickening into the wings of the last and staying on strongly to the line. Not disgraced when last seen finishing fourth, 25 lengths behind the subsequent Grade 1 winner My Drogo in the Grade 2 Premier Novices' Hurdle at Kelso, Bareback Jack starts the new season on a very attractive mark of 136. He has plenty of pace and a useful turn of foot to boot, but his pedigree suggests that he should also be suited to a step up in trip to 2m 4f.

Nick Kent has a useful horse on his hands with **Erne River**.

This Califet gelding had some strong pointing form and made a pleasing debut under Rules in a novices' hurdle over an extended 2m 6f at Kelso last November, making most of the running before dropping to third after the last in a race won by the vastly experienced Aloomomo.

Given a winter break, Erne River returned with a bang at Doncaster in an extended 2m 3f novices' hurdle. Again, he was keen to get on with things but jumped well and came clear down the home straight to record a five-length victory over Kildimo with two subsequent winners further down the field.

Confirming that was no fluke, he then made all to win under a penalty at Warwick in May, this time beating Moonlight Flit by a very easy eight lengths and earning a mark of 127 from the handicapper.

Erne River appears to love his racing. He shows real enthusiasm to get on with things and attacks his hurdles before knuckling down admirably when asked to put a race to bed. Given his experience, he could step straight into handicap company and easily have a say from what looks a workable mark. He's exciting.

Ben Pauling's **Guardino** emerged as a horse to look forward to this coming season when battling gamely to success in a bumper at Kempton in February. Prior to that he finished a good third at Carlisle in November, after which it was reported by his trainer that the horse had produced a dirty trachea wash.

By Authorized out of a Manduro mare, speed is definitely of the essence for the five-year-old and he could be one for a maiden or novices' hurdle around somewhere like Newbury, or even back at Kempton. He could be quite smart.

Kilbeg King made a late start to his career under Rules but made up for lost time by winning by an easy seven and a half lengths in the bumper on Midlands National Day at Uttoxeter in March. The Doyen gelding always travelled strongly through the race and moved through to lead over two furlongs from home before keeping on strongly up the run-in.

A half-brother to the 2m 4f chase winner Champagne Noir, a step up in trip over hurdles will suit the six-year-old. He looks a useful recruit for Anthony Honeyball.

Nicky Henderson's trio Gallyhill, Patroclus and Will Carver all achieved success in their first season under Rules.

There was plenty of expectation resting on the shoulders of **Gallyhill** when he made his Rules debut at Newbury in January, but he got the job done despite the heavy ground conditions probably being deeper than he would've liked. He then went to Ascot and ran a commendable race to finish second to the 137-rated Midnight River with the then 131-rated One True King back in third.

Pulled up when last seen at Aintree in the Grade 1 Sefton Novices' Hurdle where it was reported that he made a respiratory noise, I would imagine he'll have undergone a breathing operation over the summer and a novice chase campaign could be on the cards. He's a big, scopey individual and that's where his strengths will lie.

Patroclus was also pulled up when last seen. That was in the Grade 3 EBF Final at Sandown in March where the ground was awfully taxing and the gelding also suffered an overreach. Prior to that he'd stayed on well to win over 2m 1f at Exeter and defied a penalty in ultra-game style at Doncaster to beat Riggs with more in hand than the three parts of a length suggests.

Will Carver made hay whilst the sun shone in the spring, winning over hurdles at both Kempton and Perth in very easy fashion. Those victories have earned him a rating of 132, and whilst the form may not be too strong, it's clear that the gelding is progressing at a rapid rate of knots and can enter the chase division with plenty of confidence. His pointing form worked out well and fences have the potential to unlock further success.

Colin Tizzard's yard struggled for form throughout last season but Killer Kane, Striking A Pose and Amarillo Sky all managed to get on the board.

Amarillo Sky showed plenty of natural pace to win a point-to-point and ran OK on his first three starts over hurdles before making good use of a very lenient handicap mark of 115 at Exeter in March where he won by a very easy seven lengths from Steady Away. Not quite up to Grade 3 level when possibly failing to see out the 2m 4f trip next time at Aintree from a mark of 128, he appreciated the drop in company when landing a Class 3 handicap over 2m 1f at Newton Abbot in May and came home the 16-length winner from a mark of 125. He can still cause some damage from his new mark of 132.

Killer Kane cost a small fortune when passing through the sales ring for £300,000 and ran well to finish second on his hurdling debut at Aintree over 2m 4f last October but didn't see out his race next time at Exeter when trailing home 24 lengths behind Karl Philippe in February.

Sent back to Exeter the following month for a novices' hurdle over 2m 1f, he led the 15-runner field a merry dance after being left in front at the second flight of hurdles, jumping slickly and looking to have matters in full control entering the home straight before pulling clear under hands and heels riding after the last.

He's a smart horse and can easily defy his handicap mark of 129. I predict he'll have a big season.

Striking A Pose ran on well to finish third in a novices' hurdle over an extended 1m 7f at Ascot last October and improved considerably for a step up to an extended 2m 5f at Wincanton in December, travelling strongly and making smooth headway on the outside of the field before kicking clear between the final two flights.

He followed that with an 11-length victory over an extended 2m 2f at Exeter in February, making all and jumping nimbly before coasting clear to cross the line in a canter. Pulled up on horrible ground in the EBF Final at Sandown from a mark of 130 in March, he then finished the season after unseating his rider in the Grade 1 Betway Mersey Novices' Hurdle at Aintree.

Striking A Pose has plenty of class and he's an exciting prospect for novice chasing. Watch out for him contesting a novices' handicap chase.

Shirocco's Dream is another who can build on two promising runs over hurdles. She's a strong traveller and only needs one run to secure a handicap rating. Expect better things from her as the season progresses.

Harry Whittington's string were also stuck under a cloud last season, but **Docpickedme** found the winning groove at Southwell in March when beating a 13-runner field by a comfortable three and a half lengths. He's a genuine and uncomplicated sort of horse who stays strongly. It's worth remembering that he beat Patroclus in his point-to-point and he'll likely have more to offer from his mark of 119.

Sir Sholokhov also achieved success twice in handicap chases for owners Simon Munir & Isaac Souede having finished third on hurdling debut behind My Drogo. The six-year-old is known to suffer from wind issues and has since been sold cheaply for £8,000 at the Goffs UK September (H-I-T) Sale.

Another who was sold through the ring was **Greenrock Abbey**, who now joins Kerry Lee.

The flashy white-faced gelding was running a nice race on his hurdling debut over an extended 2m 5f at Ascot last November but suffered a crunching fall at the second from home when still holding a chance. Given plenty of time to get over that, he then went to Doncaster in March but was completely unsighted at the first hurdle and came to grief again. He rounded off his luckless season with a seventh placed effort behind Java Point at Warwick later that month.

Hopefully, he has a little more good fortune for his new connections as he has the potential to be a nice horse.

Others who look poised to make a mark in the handicap division include Upandatit, Hidden Commander, Robin Des Theatre and Elmdale.

Upandatit was given a wind operation after his Rules debut in a bumper at Musselburgh in January and hasn't troubled the judge in four subsequent starts over hurdles. However, he has shown promise in defeat, notably when running on into third behind Word Has It in a 2m novices' hurdle at Kelso in March, and he also caught the eye when staying on into fifth over two furlongs further on a return to that track the following month. He was fourth, beaten 36 lengths, when last seen at Perth in May in a 2m 4f maiden hurdle, again plugging on but never threatening. He now starts the new season on a mark of 107 and should be suited by a handicap over 2m 4f or 3m. Soft ground won't inconvenience him.

Hidden Commander has some smart pointing form, notably the one-length beating of Flame Bearer, but he hasn't put his best foot forward in six starts for Philip Kirby and is now rated on a mark of 100. That could be dangerous, especially when you view his sixth-placed effort in an extended 2m 3f at Catterick last November which drew questions from the stewards. He travelled well on the front end that day and still held every chance turning for home until tiring over the final couple of obstacles. Three subsequent runs after a wind operation leave plenty to be desired, but he retains potential and is one to keep onside.

Robin Des Theatre has been allotted an opening mark of 103 despite winning once and showing promise on her other three starts. The six-year-old daughter of Robin Des Champs was last seen finishing 17 lengths adrift of the very useful Dreams Of Home in a novices' hurdle over 2m at Newcastle in March, having won over that course and distance the previous month when beating Lady Tremaine by a neck.

Bred to stay further, she's open to further progress once she tackles fences.

Elmdale would have been up there with the biggest horse I featured in last year's book, and hurdles were never going to bring out the best in him. Given his pointing experience, I imagine he'll go straight into a novice handicap chase where he can make good use of a mark of 107. Big galloping tracks and soft ground suit him well. We haven't seen the best of him yet.

Nigel Twiston-Davies also has a nice young novice chaser to look forward to with **Poppa Poutine**. A two-time winner over hurdles over trips in excess of three miles, he's a resolute stayer and although he's only rated on a mark of 126, I wonder if he can progress into a National Hunt Chase candidate. He's certainly one for all those staying novice handicap chases.

I'm looking forward to **Pozo Emery**'s chase debut.

Paul Nicholls' gelding overcame significant greenness to win on hurdling debut over an extended 2m 3f at Chepstow in January. Running in snatches at the head of the field and taking a good look at his flights, he kept on strongly under a persistent Bryony Frost to win by one and a quarter lengths from Champagne Rhythm.

Second on his next two starts at Wincanton and on a revisit to Chepstow, he looks every inch a staying chaser and last season's experiences will not be lost on him. He's a lovely young horse.

David Pipe also has a couple of recruits nicely poised on attractive marks, including **Red Lion Lad** who won his point by a wide margin and shaped encouragingly on two of his three starts last term. He looked quite green under pressure but ought to have come on a bundle for a summer out at grass and he can easily shed his maiden tag in a handicap from a mark of 116. He looks a strong stayer and handles testing ground.

Gericault Roque is a lovely young horse who won two of his three starts over hurdles last term having shown plenty of ability on his Rules debut in a bumper at Newton Abbot. He won despite the tight turns at Plumpton in January when getting up in the shadows of the post but looked far more at home when winning by a widening nine and a half lengths at Sandown in March. That was a handicap hurdle over 2m from a mark of 117 and the handicapper hasn't reacted too harshly, only putting him up 7lb to 124. He can go in again, especially when tackling 2m 4f as he stays very well.

I had high hopes for **Maggies Mogul** at the start of the season, but she's been very disappointing since showing promise in a bumper whilst **Home Farm House** ran well for a long way at Newton Abbot in a maiden hurdle over 2m 5f but didn't get home. She has potential from a mark of 96.

Tom Lacey's **Glory And Honour** bumped into Any News and Isolate on his first two starts under Rules in bumpers but got off the mark at the third time of asking when switched to hurdles for a maiden over 2m at Huntingdon in November. Not short of pace, he then won a jumpers' bumper at Lingfield but failed to follow up in a similar contest at Newcastle when beaten three lengths by Presentandcounting. Third in handicap company on his last two starts from marks of 127 and 129, he'll likely stick to hurdles.

Dan Skelton's **Wild Romance** registered the first success for the book when scooting to a half-length debut success over hurdles at Chepstow last October. She then ran very well when closing to within three lengths of Does He Know in a Grade 2 at Cheltenham in November. A lovely honest mare, presumably she met with a setback but hopefully she can pick up from where she left off last term.

Lakota Warrior shaped with potential on his bumper debut at Warwick in December but ran poorly when sent to Kelso in February. He's a big horse and maybe just needed more time, but so far he's not shown the level of form that saw him finish a head behind Gerri Colombe in a point-to-point.

Fergal O'Brien's **Long Stay** won by nine lengths on bumper debut at Newton Abbot last September but bumped into the useful Bareback Jack on his first try over hurdles at Musselburgh in November, battling bravely but unable to stay with the winner on the run-in.

Back to winning ways later in the month, this time over 2m at Ludlow, he travelled strongly and was produced to challenge three from home before pulling clear and keeping on well on the run-in. He's a smart sort with a touch of class and could be capable of scooping a nice pot this side of Christmas.

The Philip Hobbs-trained **Orbys Legend** highlighted himself as a horse to follow when finishing second in a decent bumper at Newbury last November before making a winning start to his career over hurdles in a 2m 1f novices' contest at Exeter the following month. Unable to land a blow when third behind Martinhal on a revisit to that track in February over an extended 2m 2f, he then impressed with a 12-length victory from Morfee at Sandown in March when dropped back to two miles.

A strong traveller, he loves a bit of nice ground and should be suited to a step up in trip this term. He has the potential to continue on an upward curve and may be one for something like the Tote Silver Trophy at Chepstow at the start of the season.

All is not lost with stable companion **Across The Channel** who was far too keen when finishing last on his hurdling debut at Wetherby last October. Given plenty of time off, he ran much better in a first-time hood at Newbury in March and has the potential to improve as he matures.

Chosen Port, a sister to Burtons Well, ought to find winning opportunities when stepped up in trip over hurdles. She showed promise in bumpers but her pedigree is littered with stamina. **Ripper Roo** rounded off a consistent first-season campaign with a convincing victory in an extended 2m 4f maiden hurdle at Market Rasen in April. He's only rated on a mark of 118 and there should be loads more to come.

The same can be said for **Fabrique En France**, rated 119. A wind operation did the trick for him getting off the mark at Wincanton in January over an extended 1m 7f, but he's an imposing individual and should see out a trip. He's likely to go novice handicap chasing.

Another for novice handicap chases could be **Timeless Beauty**. A big, raw mare, she made good use of an opening handicap mark of 99 at Ayr in January when relishing the heavy ground and coming clear to beat Charm Offensive by an easy six and a half lengths. Placed on her next two starts, she should come on appreciably for her summer break and improvement over fences can be expected.

A Time To Shine quickly switched to fences after finishing third over hurdles on his first two starts under Rules. He very nearly landed a novices' handicap chase at the first time of asking at Hereford over 3m 1f from a mark of 115 but bumped into a well-handicapped Minella Bobo. He then pulled up when last seen at Warwick in March, but he's the type who will flourish for a summer out at grass and I won't be giving up on him just yet.

Harry Fry is gearing up for the season from his new base down in Dorset, where hopefully he can find the winning formula for **Fishkhov**. The six-year-old finished three parts of a length behind the subsequent Albert Bartlett Novices' Hurdle winner, Vanillier, in a point-to-point in December 2019, but has been disappointing in both a bumper and a maiden hurdle over an extended 2m 3f. He's better than that and should be noted wherever he runs first time out. Maybe he'd be more at home on a sounder surface. He'll get three miles in time.

Stable companion **Revels Hill** won a handicap hurdle over 2m 5f from a mark of 116 at Warwick towards the end of last season and can take his form to a new level in the novice handicap chase division. An imposing sort who travels strongly, he still has the potential to be above average.

Tallow For Coal has been placed on each of his three starts over hurdles and was stepped up in trip to an extended 3m 1f last time at Hereford. His best form was at Uttoxeter over 2m 4f and a return to a more galloping track may be the ticket to success. **A Distant Place** finished fourth on his debut at Newton Abbot but has been narrowly touched off on his two subsequent starts at Hereford and Leicester. He's a battler and will find his way to the winner's enclosure before long. Maybe a step up to 3m will help.

Brooksway Fair hasn't lived up to expectations and he was unable to land a solid gamble when making his handicap debut in a novices' handicap chase from a mark of 88 at Ludlow in February. He was well backed again next time at Huntingdon but trailed home 36 lengths behind the winner. A mark of 86 highlights how poorly he's run, but the win over Orbys Legend in a point-to-point in February 2020 cannot be forgotten.

Ahead Of The Field enjoyed success under Rules at the second time of asking for Sean Thomas Doyle and has now joined Emma Lavelle. He looks a really lovely prospect for the staying hurdle division and could prove to be an above average sort on some nice ground. He's a brother to Relegate and has a sparkle of class.

Kenyan Cowboy has slipped to a mark of 95 from an opening mark of 106, but he looked to have very little excuse when only third at Chepstow in a handicap hurdle over an extended 2m 3f in April. He's showed promise at that track before, so may be worth keeping an eye on if venturing back to Wales.

Fashion Nova didn't show any real spark in four subsequent starts after finishing third on her bumper debut and now has plenty to prove, although a mark of 76 over hurdles is very handy, if she can put her troubles behind her. **Feralkat** remains unexposed after only the two starts last term. She'll love deep mid-winter ground and will stay forever. **Rossbeigh Strand** was far too keen on his bumper debut at Uttoxeter last November but will be interesting over hurdles when upped in trip and is one to stick with.

At the time of writing, Glenglass, Tag Man, Minella Majestic, Lets Go Champ, Garter Lane, Fuego De L'Abbaye, Bold Conduct and Carrig Copper haven't run under Rules.

Index

Star Potential Horses appear in purple

Notes

Notes

Notes